What People Are Saying About Jeremiah J. Johnston…

This is a challenging time for Christians everywhere. I am very pleased that my good friend Jeremiah Johnston has written *Unanswered: Lasting Truth for Trending Questions,* an insightful book that will have a lasting impact on all readers. His spiritual insights make this a captivating and compelling book. You will be inspired by the truth and encouraged as you seek answers to unanswered questions in your life.

—Dr. Jay Alan Sekulow
Chief Counsel, American Center for Law & Justice

Dr. Johnston loves the truth and he loves people. In *Unanswered,* both come through clearly. He writes and communicates as a scholar with a keen mind, but also as a pastor with a compassionate heart. By God's grace, *Unanswered* will "teach Christians to become thinkers and thinkers to become Christians."

—Eric Geiger
Vice President, LifeWay Christian Resources

"*You have not because you ask not,*" said New Testament writer, James. "*Your questions are not answered because you've not yet read* Unanswered," said… me! In this fresh, intelligent book, Dr. Jeremiah Johnston (don't let the "Dr." scare you; he writes in plain English) gives great responses to some of the most daunting spiritual questions we're all curious about. My advice: 1.) Get this book (seriously, how many books do you know of that smartly discuss both the *veracity of the Bible* and *vampires?*); 2.) Read this book right away (it's too important to put in the stack with all the other ones you want to read "some day"); 3.) Give copies of this book to people you know (some of whom are just a few good answers away from a confident faith in Christ).

—Mark Mittelberg
Best-selling author of *The Questions Christians Hope No One Will Ask* and *Confident Faith*
Executive Director, The Center for American Evangelism

Intriguing...stimulating...challenging. These words represent Dr. Jeremiah Johnston's new book, *Unanswered*. It will definitely meet a huge need in today's church. Not only will it answer questions for those seeking the truth, it will also encourage the communicators of God's truth, giving them greater confidence in answering the current questions people are asking today.

—*Dr. Ronnie Floyd*
President, Southern Baptist Convention
Senior Pastor, Cross Church, Springdale, Arkansas

It is a pleasure to commend this lively and readable book. Some apologetics books are overly technical (and frankly, dull), and many fail to grapple with the current questions as framed by modern enquirers and sceptics. Not so *Unanswered*. Jeremiah Johnston writes with the heart of a pastor and the mind of a scholar. Unanswered questions—about silence, suicide, suffering, and Scripture, to name but a few—pose real problems for real people, which demand the care and compassion that this book provides. This book is accessible and credible; it is a delight to read, and I shall be giving copies away to friends who have wrestled with unanswered questions for years.

—*Reverend Dr. Simon Vibert*
Vice Principal, Director of the School of Preaching
Wycliffe Hall, University of Oxford

Unanswered is a brilliant showcase of Dr. Johnston's tremendous mind and, more importantly, his love for people and the church. In it, he tackles some of Christianity's toughest questions and gives readers, believers and nonbelievers alike, the answers they've sought. He is one of the brightest minds of our generation and I cannot recommend *Unanswered* more highly.

—*Matthew Barnett*
Cofounder, The Dream Center, Los Angeles, California
Author, *The Church That Never Sleeps*

I commend to you this new and vastly important work. Having pastored and ministered for over three decades, I have found the questions upon which Johnston focuses to be real life points of concern. Combining Scripture, common sense, solid research, and a kind heart, Johnston masterfully presents a compelling case for the powerful ministry of our Lord in real life situations. Having been in a family that has experienced mental illness and suicide, I especially appreciate his balanced treatment to these issues. This will be an important addition in the field of apologetics and pastoral ministry.

—Frank Page, Ph.D.
President and CEO, Southern Baptist Convention Executive Committee

Unanswered tackles the questions that no one talks about in the church. This is a must read for anyone who desires to deal with the difficult questions people are asking today!

—Dr. Ben Young
Author, *Why Mike's Not A Christian*
Pastor, Second Baptist Church, Houston, Texas

Jeremiah Johnston has an impressive résumé in a multitude of areas: media, biblical scholarship, apologetics, and pastoral work in a megachurch. He is also a man of almost unfathomable vision. His Christian Thinkers Society addresses our post-Christian world head-on with remarkable clarity and insight. It is vast in its concept and fills a massive gap in apologetics and biblical literacy. God has raised up Dr. Johnston for such a time as this.

—Daniel B. Wallace, Ph.D.
Professor of New Testament Studies
Dallas Theological Seminary

Not since the days of the Roman Empire have Christians faced so many challenges and attacks. Many Christians are unsure how to respond and do not know how to defend their faith. In *Unanswered,* Dr. Jeremiah Johnston offers a fresh yet striking defense of the Christian faith, providing the tools and resources essential for every believer in a post-Christian world. Christian Thinkers Society is a go-to ministry for powerful yet concise discussion and answers from some of the world's brightest minds. Its founder, Dr. Johnston, is a respected scholar whose humor and personality make the discussions engaging, even entertaining.

—*Dr. Michael Licona*
Associate Professor of Theology
Houston Baptist University

We all know someone who has walked away from the faith, tragically, because of unanswered questions and doubts. With *Unanswered,* Dr. Jeremiah Johnston offers precisely what the church needs today—tools and answers! His Christian Thinkers Society is a creative, engaging forum that truly connects with this generation. It is a ministry that reaches both seekers asking the tough faith questions as well as believers desiring to strengthen their faith. I enthusiastically support this endeavor!

—*Dr. Paul Copan*
Pledger Family Chair of Philosophy and Ethics
Palm Beach Atlantic University

Today more than ever, the Christian church needs people who are able to communicate truth in a skeptical world. Combining scholarly integrity with creative excellence, Dr. Jeremiah Johnston is giving bright minds a platform to broadcast from. I commend *Unanswered* and the Christian Thinkers Society for providing a compelling voice in a world that desperately needs to hear good news.

—*Justin Brierley*
Host of the *Unbelievable?* radio show and podcast

Theology, philosophy, and apologetics are disciplines at the heart of a flourishing Christian university. HBU's growing strength in these areas has been blessed by the addition of Dr. Jeremiah Johnston. Dr. Johnston is an exciting, up-and-coming scholar who has founded Christian Thinkers Society and is now presenting us with *Unanswered*. He has a record of sharing the gospel in a winsome and intellectually serious manner. We look forward to the growth his leadership will provide to our events and national outreach.

—*Dr. Robert B. Sloan Jr.*
President, Houston Baptist University

Jeremiah Johnston is the rare scholar who has a passion for both ministry and academics, love for both the church and the world, and is a team-builder working to promote others for the sake of the kingdom. He has a first-rate mind and a great academic pedigree. It is a pleasure to recommend *Unanswered* to you.

—*Robert B. Stewart*
Professor of Philosophy and Theology
Greer-Heard Chair of Faith and Culture
Director, Institute for Christian Apologetics
New Orleans Baptist Theological Seminary

I have known Jeremiah Johnston for many years and I am happy that the Christian Thinkers Society is now a part of Houston Baptist University, making Jeremiah's recent research available to an entirely new audience. This is a welcome partnership that I'm sure will benefit the cause of the kingdom.

—*Gary R. Habermas*
Distinguished research professor
Chair, Philosophy Department
Liberty University

It gives me great pleasure to communicate my hearty endorsement for Dr. Jeremiah Johnston and *Unanswered*. His scholarly achievements and performance in the classroom are stellar and though these achievements are superlative, I believe Jeremy has made even more significant contributions through his work of mediating the scholarship from the academy to Christian men and women in churches who have a real passion to become mature disciples. The vision that resulted in the Christian Thinkers Society was inspired, and I believe it has the potential to transform and enrich the faith of Christians on a global level. I believe he is leading the vanguard of a new movement that is creating a robust and academically rigorous apologetic that will have a huge impact on the shape of contemporary Christianity, and who knows, perhaps the passage of time will show this to be a significant moment in the history of the church, not just in the US but as a truly worldwide movement.

—*Dr. Paul Foster*
Head of School of Divinity
University of Edinburgh

Through *Unanswered* and the Christian Thinkers Society, Dr. Jeremiah Johnston continues to make a strong case for the veracity of the Christian worldview. If you're seeking the truth, or just learning how to be a better Christian case-maker, Dr. Johnston's work will be an encouragement and blessing.

—*J. Warner Wallace*
Cold-case homicide detective
Adjunct Professor of Apologetics, Biola University
Author, *Cold-Case Christianity*, *Alive*, and *God's Crime Scene*

Dr. Jeremiah Johnston is a pastor and scholar whose desire is to bring the best of scholarship to the church in an accessible way. *Unanswered* tackles hard questions head-on. I warmly commend it!

—*Dr. Peter J. Williams*
Warden, Tyndale House, Cambridge, UK

The ministry of Jeremiah Johnston and the Christian Thinkers Society tackles the questions and challenges facing Christians in our increasingly skeptical culture. Through equipping leaders, training believers, and providing timely resources, CTS provides the apologetic tools needed to grow the body of Christ and engage today's culture in a winsome and informed way.

—*Brian Auten*

Founder and President, Apologetics 315

Dr. Jeremiah Johnston has written just the book that today's generation desperately needs. The polls indicate that people are dropping out of church but not losing interest in the big questions about God and faith. Many have become disenchanted with the church because pressing questions are not being addressed, let alone answered. In *Unanswered* Dr. Johnston tackles head-on the tough questions. He provides thought provoking, well-reasoned answers in a way that all readers will appreciate and understand. It is a pleasure for me to recommend this book. I urge everyone to read it!

—*Craig A. Evans*

John Bisagno Distinguished Professor of Christian Origins
Houston Baptist University

We live in a radically skeptical age. Far too few people are able to make an effective case for Christianity at the highest levels. Dr. Johnston is a breath of fresh air in this regard. He can answer the toughest questions skeptics are asking about faith in Christ—and he does it in a deeply engaging and attractive way. *Unanswered* is proof of his special ability to mobilize believers and equip them with new and effective methods of proclaiming and defending the gospel of the Lord Jesus Christ in an age that seems to get darker and darker. His Christian Thinkers Society is a stroke of genius and we need to see it multiplied across our country and beyond. The work of Dr. Johnston is clear evidence the Lord is on the move—it all fills me with very bright hope.

—*Dr. Craig J. Hazen*

Founder and Director, Graduate Program in Christian Apologetics
Founder and Director, Graduate Program in Science and Religion
Biola University
Author, *Five Sacred Crossings*

I have known Dr. Jeremiah Johnston since he was a young associate pastor of a thriving church. I have watched with increasing interest as he has developed into one of the leading Christian apologists of our time. His long-awaited book, *Unanswered: Lasting Truth for Trending Questions,* is one of the most strategic books on apologetics to appear in recent years. It is a mine of information on questions often overlooked by other books on apologetics. The book was borne out of years of personal research, thus it avoids an ivory-tower approach to the subject. Dr. Johnston has done the evangelical cause—and especially the youth of this generation—a great service by writing this book.

—*Dr. Harold Rawlings*
Assistant Director, The Rawlings Foundation, Florence, Kentucky
Author, *Trial By Fire*

Looking for answers to some of the tough questions your skeptical friends ask about the Christian faith? Wrestling with questions yourself? Know a friend who has walked away from Christianity and want to help them? If any of those situations apply to you, you're going to find this an immensely helpful book. Combining philosophical insight with pastoral wisdom and a gift for careful communication, Jeremiah Johnston tackles some of the toughest apologetic questions with insight, depth, and compassion. Every church and every Christian needs apologetics if they're to engage the culture with the gospel. This book is a terrific resource for that missional task.

—*Dr. Andy Bannister*
Canadian Director, Ravi Zacharias International Ministries
Author, *The Atheist Who Didn't Exist*

Unanswered is an inviting work in apologetics. Jeremiah's practical advice is gracious, straightforward, and accessible. In fact, he is the first apologist I have encountered to use phrases in his work such as "Don't go into Beast Mode" and "chillaxe"! His writing demonstrates a deep passion for ministering to others out of the truth of Scripture. Jeremiah is convicted, as am I, that apologetics is an instrumental part of the Christian life. Apologetics is not solely for acquiring propositional knowledge to answer the objections about God. Rather, apologetics can also serve personal transformation, as Christians begin to more fully comprehend and experience the reality of God.

—*Mary Jo Sharp*
Assistant Professor of Apologetics, Houston Baptist University
Director, Confident Christianity

Every Christian is called to be able to give a defense for the hope that is within us. Jeremiah Johnston's *Unanswered* will help believers in the Lord Jesus Christ to do just that. I highly recommend *Unanswered* for every Christian who wants to be better equipped "*to contend earnestly for the faith which was once for all delivered to the saints*" (Jude 3 NKJV).

—*Dr. Jason Allen*
President, Midwestern Baptist Theological Seminary

Scripture challenges, "*Be diligent to present yourself approved to God, a worker who does not need to be ashamed, rightly dividing the word of truth*" (2 Timothy 2:15 NKJV). Nobody knows a son like his father. For ten years I have watched Jeremiah teach effectively in the local church while simultaneously going through the rigors of theological academic instruction at the feet of some of the best scholars, by the grace of God; he *accurately* proclaims the word of truth with God-given, Spirit-anointed communication skills. Using this book and the accompanying study will fill your church to capacity with eager listeners, the lost *will* come to Christ, and believers will be empowered to become articulate to share their faith.

—*Dr. Jerry Johnston*
www.jerryjohnston.com

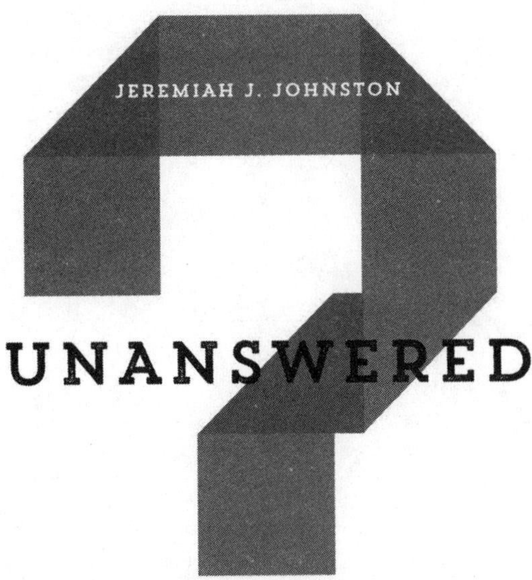

JEREMIAH J. JOHNSTON

UNANSWERED

LASTING TRUTH FOR TRENDING QUESTIONS

JEREMIAH J. JOHNSTON

UNANSWERED

LASTING TRUTH FOR TRENDING QUESTIONS

WHITAKER HOUSE

UNANSWERED:
Lasting Truth for Trending Questions

Christian Thinkers Corporation
8019 W. Grand Parkway S.
Ste. 1060-416
Richmond, Texas 77407
www.ChristianThinkers.com
Jeremiah@ChristianThinkers.com

ISBN: 978-1-62911-656-3
eBook ISBN: 978-1-62911-657-0
Printed in the United States of America

Whitaker House
1030 Hunt Valley Circle
New Kensington, PA 15068
www.whitakerhouse.com

Library of Congress Cataloging-in-Publication Data

Johnston, Jeremiah, author.
Unanswered : lasting truth for trending questions / by Jeremiah J. Johnston Ph.D.
pages cm
Includes bibliographical references.
Summary: "Dr. Jeremiah Johnson addresses six categories of recurring, trending questions that plague the minds of believers but are rarely addressed in church"— Provided by publisher.
ISBN 978-1-62911-656-3 (trade pbk. : alk. paper) — ISBN 978-1-62911-657-0 (ebook) 1. Christianity—Miscellanea. I. Title.
BR96.J64 2015
230—dc23
2015033699

1 2 3 4 5 6 7 8 9 10 11 **w** 22 21 20 19 18 17 16 15

For Audrey,
Together we are one,
always and forever.

CONTENTS

FOREWORD

I've always been brimming with curiosity. As a child I peppered my parents with so many questions that they finally bought me an encyclopedia, and said, "Read this! The answers are in here." Yes, some of them were, but not the deeper ones that I began to ponder as I got older.

Is religion based on myths and fables? If God exists, why doesn't He make Himself more obvious to us? How could a loving God allow so much suffering in the world? Isn't the Bible filled with contradictions and bad history? Is the resurrection of Jesus credible? Hasn't science trumped faith? Isn't Christianity narrow-minded and intolerant? Where does morality come from?

The Christians I knew earlier in my life didn't want to discuss these things. Basically, I was told to keep quiet. My conclusion: there must not be any good answers, or else they would be willing to engage with me on these issues. Thus, my road to atheism was paved by unanswered questions.

My agnostic wife's conversion to Christianity, and the resulting positive changes in her character and values, prompted me to use my journalism and legal background to investigate the credibility of Christianity. After nearly two years of seeking answers, I became convinced that science and history point powerfully toward the truth of the Christian faith. I received Jesus as my Forgiver and Leader in 1981.

But guess what? The questions didn't stop!

Why are so many of my prayers unanswered? If God has a plan for my life, why doesn't He make it clearer? Why doesn't God simply remove my sinful desires? Why are there times that God feels so distant from me?

What I've come to learn is simple: Questions are good—as long as answers are sincerely pursued. In fact, the world is in desperate need of Christians who are able to intelligently discuss these topics with spiritual seekers and fellow believers—and to do so, as 1 Peter 3:15 says, "*with gentleness and respect.*" We ought to emulate Jesus, who didn't flinch at questions from anyone who was honestly seeking truth.

That's why this new book by my friend and Houston Baptist University colleague Jeremiah J. Johnston is so important. His experience with Christian Thinkers Society has exposed him to hundreds of questions that are roadblocks to seekers or stumbling blocks for Christians. He has culled through these objections in order to provide solid answers and analysis to *real* questions being asked by *real* people.

This is a winsome and accessible book, drawing from Jeremiah's considerable academic training, his pastoral work in the trenches of ministry, and his deeply felt passion to reach people with truth while equipping others to do the same. His analysis is unflinching, his approach is practical, and his writing is clear—a great combination!

Whether you personally wrestle with objections or not, the chances are that you will encounter friends and family members who are authentically searching for answers to the big questions of life. Let Jeremiah prepare you to be purveyors of truth and hope to an increasingly skeptical world.

Be prepared to think...and to grow.

—Lee Strobel
Author, *The Case for Christ* and *The Case for Faith*
Professor, Houston Baptist University

1

QUESTIONS HAVE POWER

An Invitation

Questions have power; unanswered questions linger. Questions will lead to freedom; unanswered questions can entrap. Questions multiply and require something of us. The longer an unanswered question lurks the more it erodes the confidence to trust in something. Within the church today there exists a deepening chasm of unanswered questions consuming more and more potential "ex-Christians." Most of us know someone who has walked away from the faith, tragically, because they could not escape the quicksand of an unanswered question. Serious unanswered questions have crept into the church and it has, for the most part, failed to countermeasure with accessible answers. On the rare occasions when the church attempts to answer an unanswered question, why does it feel so awkward? When we endeavor to speak to the issues of our time, why does it look more like we are diffusing a bomb and less like we are administering an antidote? More often than not, difficult questions are considered to be hazardous waste in the church, which must be dealt with quickly and quietly. In reality, a church that ignores unanswered questions is a church that foments despair, which can lead to individual skepticism and wholesale disbelief.

I will never forget when Sarah, who had grown up in the church, told me about her negative experience with an unanswered question. Using the language of a street gang, she summarized the uncaring approach of her church's response as an "ambush" and "drive-by shooting." She was told, "Don't ask; just believe." She perceived that her church did not even pretend to care about her protracted struggle with doubt. Since when did questioning the Christian faith become a sin? Jesus certainly questioned the religious establishment of His day—*His* religious establishment. Indeed, Jesus asked a myriad of questions. Jesus' personality is impressed on His church, which is not a rickety house of cards, unable to absorb the trending questions of the day. Rather, the Christian faith is open to investigation, buttressed by overpowering evidence and an explanatory power that speaks to, and provides answers for, the deepest yearnings of the heart. That is the church I know. That is the church I was reared in and that I love. I have served the church for as long as I can remember, but the church is not perfect, nor is it designed to be. The church is organic and, at significant moments in history, has undergone self-correction. The church is not an edifice but a people, indeed, a family. It is a people God created in His own image with the freedom and ability to think, to act, and, ultimately, to question.

Having received over four thousand questions via text at our Christian Thinkers Society (CTS) events over a span of six years (2009–2015), I became acutely aware of the need to write *Unanswered: Lasting Truth for Trending Questions*. Christians of all stripes, across the denominational spectrum, submitted questions to CTS—*and they were not shy*. Being a Southern Baptist, I was honored to be invited to address a Missouri-Synod

Lutheran church in Dallas in 2012, with nearly one thousand people in attendance at a midweek event. I am not sure why it was at this church in particular, or why it had not dawned on me before, but I began to notice recurrent, or "trending," questions asked at our CTS events and broadcasts. These trending questions were not of the politically charged, polarizing variety that you might expect, either. For example, in chapter 8, "Elephant in the Room," I describe the astonished look I always receive when I report that the most asked question I have received relates to suicide and related "invisible diseases." Six recurrent questions dominated the inbox and led us to aggregate them into the six parts of this book, which are:

Part 1: God on Mute: What Do I Do When God Is Silent?

Part 2: Body of Proof: Why Can I Trust in the Bodily Resurrection of Jesus and How Does That Change Things Today?

Part 3: My Invisible Disease: What Christians Must Understand About Suicide and Mental Health

Part 4: Paranormalcy: Understanding the Paranormal Allure Among Christians and How to Escape It

Part 5: Bible–*ish* Christianity: Why Most Christians Know Just Enough About the Bible to Be Dangerous

Part 6: Becoming Job: Why Suffering, Me-Centric Christianity, and a Concierge-God Don't Mix

These questions are not on the periphery, nor are they merely sidebar issues in our churches. They are front and center, and often unaddressed. These unanswered questions are so complex and difficult that many Christians do not even know where to begin to find answers. Please do not be overwhelmed. In the years leading up to this publication, I have had hundreds of conversations and conducted thorough research so that you don't have to. Even so, this book is not meant to be a be-all and end-all. It is a launch point. Recent tragic events within the church (the completed suicide of Rick Warren's son, Matthew, as well as a host of other suicides among Christian pastors) and outside the church (the hit movie *American Sniper,* dealing with post-traumatic stress disorder) have brought these taboo subjects into sharper focus. Contributing to the confusion is the fact that we live in a time of information immediacy. There is a lot of bad information only a few clicks away that add barriers to the conversation—for example, the notion that an "authentic" Christian cannot complete suicide and if they do they go straight to hell. I think it goes without saying but if not, Google can be counterproductive when attempting to answer these questions within a biblical framework. Regrettably, Scripture twisting is rampant in our misinformation-saturated society. You must be discerning. After several CTS events and broadcasts, I began to wonder if leaders in the church were actually aware how prominent and widespread these unanswered questions were among Christians? After reaching out to other Christian leaders I realized that our experience at CTS, albeit not exhaustive, was representative of what scores of other churches were facing. In a hyper-connected world, we have lost contact with the real questions resounding within our churches.

One of my favorite actors, Steve Carrell, was the commencement speaker at Princeton in 2012. In his brief, fifteen-minute address, he highlighted all the ways in which the world had changed since he was in college. He recalled an instance when he suffered the rejection of actually asking out a girl in person rather than texting her to hilariously underscore how technology has impeded our ability to meaningfully connect with one another. "When I was in college, if we didn't know something, we didn't Google it; we just made an educated guess, or we made it up. We pretended that we knew, and that was good enough!" Inherent within his comments was the notion that all of the technological advances, for all the good they have done, have been isolating. As I watched Steve's presentation, I couldn't help but think of all the questions in the church. Our church members, for all their friending, followers and connections they have in the virtual world, are more detached than ever. Sadly, the church is winded, out of shape, and has fallen behind in the race to reach and influence hearts and minds.

It became apparent to me that Christian bookshelves were "answer-lite" when it came to addressing the latent unanswered questions *within* the church. There is, in fact, an abundance of riches published by modern Christian apologists addressing the questions of atheists, agnostics, seekers, and other self-described nonbelievers *outside* the church. For all that, there are comparatively few resources for followers of Jesus (including pastors), who, if they are transparent, often struggle to understand and answer their own ever-present questions. As we will see in the pages that follow, the sad reality is that fellow believers—our brothers and sisters in Christ—make destructive decisions every day because of unanswered questions. Within this tension is an unprecedented ministry opportunity for this book.

I do not claim to have all of the answers. Rather, the purpose of this book is to begin a healthy discussion in the church. In an effort to land on solid conclusions and provide helpful answers to these commonly-asked questions, I have stood on the shoulders of some exceptional research and studies, which you will find notated at the end of this book should you desire to drill deeper. I am also indebted to scores of Christians and pastors on church and university campuses for their transparency and courage in raising the flag on these unanswered questions. CTS recently sponsored an event with my friend, Mark Lanier, at Houston Baptist University, my home base and where Christian Thinkers Society is a resident institute. During a ten-minute segment for open Q&A, more than three hundred questions were texted. There is a hunger to find the answers and my prayer is that this book will provide the needed sustenance.

Teaching Christians to Become Thinkers and Thinkers to Become Christians

It is an exciting time to be a Christian, but in many ways it is also more difficult. Not since the days of the Roman Empire have Christians faced so many attacks and challenges to their faith. Yet Jesus of Nazareth has never been more popular, proven by the fact that there are more Jesus followers today than ever before, expanding at a rate of seventy thousand new converts per day.[1]

Within this delicate balance I followed the calling of God to launch Christian Thinkers Society within the cut and thrust of a world becoming increasingly secular, but also more pluralistic—strikingly similar to the first-century world that gave rise to nascent Christianity. CTS is a ministry serving the church, dedicated to inspire Christians and pastors to become thinkers, and thinkers to become Christians.

The church has been reticent to tackle the trending, unanswered questions posed by people in our pews, avoiding the intersection of culture and the Bible. Every generation faces challenges—a crucial calling of their time. We are no different. For Christians today, a great and urgent challenge lies in this: many believers know little of the Bible and still less of theology—the "first things of faith." On their journeys through life, they meet skeptics who object to Christianity. Yet knowing little of the Bible and its guiding tenants, let alone its story, and failing the biblical call to *"always be ready to give a defense"* (1 Peter 3:15 NKJV), they find themselves unready and ill-equipped to explain why they believe what they believe. What is more, many Christians—particularly those in the age group of 18–34—are falling away from faith, becoming what the media refers to as "nones" (no religious belief).

Amid this disconcerting data, perhaps the most worrisome and persistent trend is that of growing biblical illiteracy among North American youth raised in church settings. Knowing little of Christianity and its great Sourcebook, their faith and commitment withers, like a vine deprived of refreshing water, good soil, and sunlight. Over time, they become "deconverted"—a tragic scenario, too often repeated. CTS is not only committed to turning back the tide of biblical illiteracy, but we are also committed to responding to the frequent literary vandalism and misrepresentation of the Bible, which can pull our faith into a cultural melee.

Yet, amid these daunting challenges, one fact remains: people are hungry for substantive answers to their questions and doubts. CTS is a ministry at the forefront of fostering biblical literacy—deeply committed to following Christ's call for believers to love the Lord with all their heart, soul, and mind. (See Matthew 22:37.) At the same time, seeking friendship with all questioners and skeptics, CTS thoughtfully challenges them to "doubt their doubts." The two-fold mission of CTS is this: to commend "first things of faith" *within* the church, and to offer cogent "reasons for hope" to those *outside* the church. Through a compelling array of interactive events, cutting-edge technology, and the leadership of gifted, caring speakers, CTS is committed to one central goal: to create a respectful setting in which atheists, agnostics, seekers, and believers can feel safe to ask life's greatest questions. Therefore, I have dedicated my life to attempting to answer the unanswered questions within our faith.

Christians Are "Mentally Ill" and "Need a Psychiatrist"

The need for this book was never more apparent to me than after our CTS team filmed an interview with Professor Peter Atkins, (retired) lecturer of chemistry at the University of Oxford and Fellow of Lincoln College. A dear personal friend of Dr. Richard Dawkins, Peter wrote the quintessential textbook on chemistry and his writings are used on scores of campuses around the globe. The focus of our film was to document the rise of the "nones" phenomena. Professor Atkins is an ardent atheist who said that "people who invite Jesus into their hearts are probably mentally ill," though he qualified it by saying he was not their psychiatrist. Nonetheless, we asked Peter what his reaction was to knowing that his lectures on critical thinking had dismantled the faith of some believers, he responded, "It gives me exceeding pleasure." Peter also concluded that "Jesus, if He even existed, was probably gay, because He spent so much time with other men" and that Jesus had an archaic and warped view of women. As a Gospels scholar, I take issue with these comments, of course. Though we disagree with his conclusions, it should be noted that Professor Atkins was a most gracious host to our crew and quite willing to share his views. (See chapter 18 "The Problem of Love" for a similar experience with our CTS crew filming at the 2015 National American Atheist Convention in Memphis, Tennessee.)

A serious concern that I have is that many Christians have their heads in the sand (see chapter 19 "Avoid Island Fever") and are so isolated that they are unaware of how people think who don't follow Jesus. Many are ignorant of what is being said about Christianity in culture. Another purpose of this book is to assist you in understanding these questions in their full context. We face major challenges today. Here is the culture's message to you as a Christian: "There is no God...*Stupid!*" The second message the culture is peddling is: "Jesus wasn't raised from the dead. There is nothing special about Him. He was married with a wife, kids, and a mortgage. Later, other people who did not know Him turned Him into a divine being, and Emperor Constantine chose the books of the Bible!"

So the Christian faith is being attacked at two central, or cardinal, teachings: namely, the belief in God, and second, the conviction that God acted decisively through the Messiah, Jesus Christ, His Son, and through His resurrection from the dead. I would not have believed it had I not seen it with my own eyes. Richard Dawkins was interviewed on CNN's *Anderson Cooper 360* on April 17, 2008. Dawkins, the entrenched atheist and author of *The God Delusion,* was discussing atheism with the host Anderson Cooper. At one point Cooper cocked his head back while laughing derisively, and asked, "How could anyone be so stupid?" He was talking about *us*. He was calling those of us who believe in God stupid. I could not believe the disrespect and discourtesy, no matter what he privately believes, laughing at "stupid" Christians. Anderson continued the interview by referencing that the Bible discusses a talking snake. These kind of comments slide right by in our post-Christian society. A vulgar *Paper* magazine article, "Free to Be Miley," documented how Miley Cyrus was raised a Christian but now claimed to be "enlightened." In reference to the Bible, Miley said, "That's f--king insane," adding, "we've outgrown that fairy tale, like we've outgrown f--king Santa and the tooth fairy."[2] In recent years, millennials who grew up watching Miley portray the wholesome Hannah Montana on TV have had to witness her descent into Hannah Montana gone wild.

A battle is raging for the hearts and minds of people all around us. There is ample confusion, yet the scales of truth tip in our favor. There is more evidence available today to prove the claim of Christianity than in any other time in our history. You have more access to information about the Christian faith than did the great Christian leaders of our past. The great preacher Charles Spurgeon knew nothing of the Dead Sea Scrolls (they were not discovered until the mid-twentieth century), and St. Augustine did not have access to the external confirmations of biblical history which was still entombed in the ground and would not to be excavated for hundreds of years. Those men trusted and thrived in their faith. We are in a golden age of Christianity in which you have a treasure-trove of wisdom and knowledge at your fingertips, which you can use to develop right thinking and vibrant faith, supported by layers of evidence that prove Jesus was who He said He was and achieved all we read that He achieved.

Therefore, we must be aware of what our culture is asking of our faith and we must be prepared to demonstrate why Christianity is believable, acceptable, worthy of our trust and obedience, and overall, a force for good in the world. *Unanswered* is dedicated to you, in the hope that it will provide you with the tools and answers essential for communicating truth to an increasingly skeptical world. The aim of this book is to equip you to speak in an informed and responsible way about the deepest questions that lie at the heart of our modern Christian faith, as a thoughtful ambassador of the Lord, radiating the abundant life of Jesus Christ. These data points identify pressing challenges—but also unique opportunities. Clearly, there is a crying need for churches throughout America to biblically educate people—young people, as well as other age groups. Even though the need is great, the resources available to meet this need have never been greater.

Unanswered: The Journey Begins

Tough questions are being asked about Christianity—inside and outside of the church. Recently one of my students said, "Questions are great, but only if you know the answers!" As I've stated, many in today's church do not know the Bible as well as they should, and people outside the church hardly know it all. Consequently, Christians are ill-equipped to provide the answers our culture and communities desperately need. Christians struggle with their own "big questions" about the faith and don't know where to turn for answers. Hence, *Unanswered* is a book to be studied as much as it is to be read. There is courage in closing in on the "unanswered" questions with the strength and confidence that springs from being able to respond in a biblically-sound and culturally-sensitive way.

To that end, in partnership with LifeWay Christian Resources, I have produced a companion Bible study that I encourage you to integrate into your time with this book. The study is one hundred twenty-eight pages and features six weeks of daily, encouraging personal Bible study that correlate with the six questions we are addressing in this book. Furthermore, there is an associated teaching DVD, also created by LifeWay, in which I speak directly to these unanswered questions. The DVD can be viewed by an individual or used by groups for in a collective Bible study venue. This book, and the companion resources, has been designed to be both proactive and reactive—reactive with respect to new developments, discoveries, and challenges represented by the unanswered questions within our churches; proactive in providing answers while articulating and clarifying important biblical truths and the evidences that confirm them. The mission of the *Unanswered* series is to provide the essential training to transform and enrich believers, Christian leaders, and pastors, who will be characterized by a thinking faith, capable to communicate confidently, and committed to escape the tendency to offer trite answers to the unanswered questions of a skeptical world.

PART 1

GOD ON MUTE: WHAT DO I DO WHEN GOD IS SILENT?

2

COME OUT, COME OUT, WHEREVER YOU ARE, GOD

Does it ever feel like God has "unfollowed" you in your life? Have you ever sensed God was playing a game of hide-and-go-seek with you? It is anything but fun. It can even seem to be a cruel, cosmic time-out—a heavenly ignore. God's hiddenness can be isolating. In visiting and speaking in churches of all denominations across North America, I have noticed that a majority of Christians are uncomfortable when another believer makes a mystical comment, such as, "God spoke ________ to me," because they have never *personally* experienced a similar sort of thing in their own lives. The apparent silence of God is a common unanswered question. Many people deal with it, few are brave enough to discuss it hypothetically, and rarely is it addressed publicly or personally.

In church after church, long-time Jesus followers are attempting to recover that sweet experience with God they remember from their past—perhaps a summer youth camp when they felt "totally sold out to God." It was much simpler then, so it seems. You are not the first Christian facing the juxtaposition of maturing in your faith, yet sensing God is further from you. As we shall see, the reality is God's silence is real, biblical, personal, common, and dare I say, not always a bad thing. This principle is not something I learned in a seminar, rather it was reality for me and my beloved wife.

Audrey, my wife, is a saint in human skin. In the fifteen years of our relationship, I cannot think of a single moment in which she has been a stumbling block to my walk with Christ. In fact, she is one of those rare people you meet who makes you want to be more like God, not because of what she says but by how she lives her life. We first met at church youth camp in Panama City Beach, Florida. She was seventeen and, on the final night of camp, she sensed God's call on her life to full-time Christian service. She went on to earn a B.A. in Biblical Studies and a Master of Divinity from our local seminary. This background is important for what I am about to say.

My wife and I experienced nearly five years of God's silence.

To be clear, that's 1,800 days, 43,000 hours, more than 2 million minutes of the deafening silence of God.

We always wanted children. We never could have dreamed that two healthy people, who loved God with all of their hearts, would be unable to conceive a child. This nightmare became our reality. Fast-forward a year or two into the silence. Pastoring a large church didn't help our situation. Some Sundays were difficult for Audrey to even attend church, which can be awkward when your husband is one of the pastors. Singing "I Am a Friend of God" was not helpful. After services, people would ask, "Are you pregnant yet?"

Are. You. Pregnant. Yet?

It seemed to be on the mind of every church member we encountered. (Loving people, by the way, who were truly and sincerely concerned and praying for us.) Nevertheless, if you have ever dealt with the emotional pain of infertility, you know it is deeply personal and most often difficult to discuss in polite conversation.

As weeks turned into months and months turned into years, that question became a weekly reminder that we were not pregnant, as if we needed to be reminded. I am not sure I will ever know the half of what my wife felt. I only know it hurt—deeply. One can probably imagine what happened next. Kind-hearted and well-meaning church members shared every possible urban legend, old wives' tale, and home remedy to help us get pregnant:

"Try this method."

"Use this blanket!"

"I saw this miracle herb on Facebook."

"Perhaps you need to pray more."

Because, of course, Audrey and I were probably not doing everything imaginable and possible to get pregnant—wink-wink.

While I cannot speak for Audrey, my personal low point came when a charismatic minister "spoke a word over us" and "had a vision" that within one year we would have a child. Needless to say, a year later I became quite skeptical of unsolicited visions and words from the Lord. There is a reason that Jesus referred to His followers as "sheep." Jesus comparing Christians to sheep was not a compliment. Sheep are some of the dumbest of all creatures and sometimes, Christians are a stark reminder of that fact by their words and actions.

We spent what, to a pastor, would equate to a small fortune having every hormone in our bodies checked. Every intimate detail of our love life was examined for medical inquiry. The physical stress paled in comparison to the emotional toll infertility was having on our marriage. At the zenith of our infertility it was so stressful we needed a vacation from it all. I took Audrey for a much needed getaway. The only problem was when we finally arrived at the hotel pool, nearly every other woman Audrey's age was pregnant. There is a reason why, after successfully having a baby, fertility clinics do not permit you to bring the new baby to visit the staff, nurse, and doctors. So emotional is the toll that even seeing the success of a fellow patient can be debilitating and cause more anxiety, which can prevent pregnancy. Needless to say, Audrey returned promptly to the hotel room from the pool. We could not escape it.

According to the *Merriam-Webster Dictionary, despair* is defined as "to no longer have any hope or belief that a situation will improve or change."[3] I think we had reached that point after nearly five years of God's deafening silence in regard to the inability to have children of our own.

May I transparently share with you what my prayers sounded like during those four years?

Lord, am I not believing enough?

Is there some sin in my life hindering You from answering?

God, You have promised us blessing. God, You have promised to withhold no good thing from those who do what is right. (See Psalm 84:11.)

God, in what way are we wrong? In what way have I sinned that You will not hear me?

Please God, if You would only show us we would change it immediately. God, we want a child. God, help us!

God, are You even listening? Your Word says You are near to the brokenhearted but You seem so far away from us now.

Perhaps you have uttered a similar prayer—or desired to. It is okay to pray like this. All of my advanced degrees in theology were of little help to me at that time. Preaching regularly in a growing church did not give me "special access" to God. For all practical purposes, Audrey and I thought God had put us in timeout, and we had no idea why.

Have you ever felt like God put you in timeout? Have you ever felt like God was on mute? The question became could we trust Him? Did we trust Him? *Would* we trust Him? Would we have the courage to allow this trial, and the associated adversities, draw us closer to God and each other?

Then, in December 2007, Audrey and I felt convicted to take our trust in God to a deeper level, trusting unreservedly on His control over our situation. We gathered each day and prayed carefully through our struggle. We came to a point of having total peace with God, no matter what

He decided. In August 2008, we were on a spiritual retreat and decided to study passages in the Bible related to trusting God. We had an overwhelming sense that we were going to return home and become pregnant with our first child. Early one morning in October of that year Audrey took a home pregnancy test. Those pregnancy tests had become a constant reminder of "NO!" to us. After five years of "NO!" my wife could barely walk through the aisle of a pharmacy without seeing a home pregnancy test and being reminded that nothing had worked. However, that particular October morning was different! I remember Audrey running toward me in our bedroom, collapsing in my arms, and saying, "It said yes!" Nine months later, my wife gave birth to our child of promise, Lily Faith, who now also has a little brother, Justin! God reminded us that He was, and still is, *El Shaddai*—Almighty God!

We hope that our story will remind you that when we cannot see the hand of God, we must trust the heart and character of God. When I fail to understand why things go the way they go in my life, I must remember that God sees the end from the beginning and He wants me to trust Him!

Audrey and I prayed and journaled throughout that period of God's silence, and we recognized that He taught us four principles for how we should respond when God seems silent and distant.

God's Silence Is Biblical, Personal, Common, and Not Always a Bad Thing

An errant understanding of God produces an inconsistent spiritual life. Bad theology inculcates incorrect thinking. There is an erroneous understanding within the church that God's silence equals His chastisement in our life. Of course, *chastisement* is a word we rarely hear in modern "Churchianity" today, but it is found in the Bible. Chastisement is the experience of God's discipline in our lives. God's silence and God's chastisement are very different things, and certainly not synonymous. If God is silent to us, it does not automatically mean that He is disciplining us. Recall the episode in John's gospel in which Jesus saw a blind man and His own disciples queried, "*Rabbi, who sinned, this man or his parents, that he was born blind?*" (John 9:2). Jesus' answer corrected the errant theology of first-century Judaism (and some modern Christianity), "*It was not that this man sinned, or his parents, but that the works of God might be displayed in him*" (verse 3). Jewish families in the first century who suffered with handicaps, birth defects, or special needs were considered outcasts. I am sure they felt God was distant. However, as we learn in John 9, God had a greater plan for this particular family to experience the power of God with healing and deliverance. God's silence is not always linked to sin.

If you are experiencing the silence of God, do not believe the lie that you are a second-tier, second-rate Christian. In reality, it is possible, even probable, that it means quite the opposite. God has entrusted you with His apparent silence for a greater reason. Trust is the central issue that needs your focus. Will you trust God to straighten out this mess in your life? Will you trust God to see you through the desert? Will you trust God, even when He says *no* or *wait* or *not now*?

The Bible is a time machine, a portal to the historical past, providing access to examples of common men and women transcending extremely difficult moments with profound courage and faith. As we search the Scriptures for answers to the unanswered questions, we must remember the Bible is history, not mythology. The stories of the Bible exhibit *verisimilitude* with the reality of the world in which the stories take place. In Latin *veritas* (root is *ver*, meaning "veracity, verifiable") means genuine or true; *similitude* means similar or likeness. Therefore, as historians and biblical scholars, when we say the New Testament exhibits verisimilitude with the first century, we are noting that the contents of the biblical narrative correspond with what we know of the era the document describes. In other words, the Bible finds its place in the ongoing cut and thrust of history and there is tremendous overlap when one compares the sacred Judeo-Christian manuscripts with other extant documents, inscriptions, and archeological findings from antiquity. We can have an abundance of confidence that the Bible speaks of real people in real places, with real ceremonial and cultural customs, who are trusting God through the vicissitudes of life. Accordingly, have you considered that God's silence is ***biblical?*** It is usually a surprise to the casual reader of the Bible that several of the major Bible characters faced moments of deafening silence from God.

The narrative of Abram and Sarai (later to become Abraham and Sarah) serve as a series of mountain-peak passages in the Old Testament. In studying the carefully recorded chronology of Abraham's life in Genesis 12–18, these seven chapters serve as a window into the twenty-five most important years of his family's life. We learn that Abram and Sarai experienced nearly twenty-five years of God's silence. The first period was ten years (see Genesis 12–16), and the second period was thirteen additional years (see Genesis 17–18). Even God's closest friends are not exempt from experiencing God's silence: *"The Scripture was fulfilled that says, 'Abraham believed God, and it was counted to him as righteousness'—and he was called a friend of God"* (James 2:23).

Abram and his family endured not one but two distinct periods of God's silence. When we encounter Abram and Sarai in the early pages of God's story they are quite ordinary. Even so, against all odds, they are able to exhibit faith in God with reckless abandon. After all, Abram, along with this family, trusted in this personal God, *Yahweh* ("I Am"), which means the self-existent One, and relocated to a new region called Canaan. If you read too quickly through Genesis 11:27–12:4, you will miss the fact that when Abram responded to God's call on his life, he left behind his heritage, his rightful land, his extended family, and all of his eventual inheritance to follow *Yahweh* 1,500 miles (2,400 km) from Ur (modern-day Iraq), through Haran (modern-day Syria), to Canaan (modern-day Israel). At his defense before the Sanhedrin, Stephen said, *"Brothers and fathers, hear me. The God of glory appeared to our father Abraham when he was in Mesopotamia, before he lived in Haran, and said to him, 'Go out from your land and from your kindred and go into the land that I will show you'"* (Acts 7:2–3). Hundreds of miles from their cultural home, Abram and Sarai found themselves in a foreign land, aging and childless.

Not only is God's silence biblical, it is also ***personal.*** How is that? God's silence is personal because it can be the agent of our transformation. In Genesis 12, Abram ("great father") was a pagan, he was seventy-five years old when God asked him to leave everything he knew to follow Him. God promised Abram, *"I will make of you a great nation"* (Genesis 12:2). For many Christians it is not difficult to identify with the experience of God's silence. While it might not be the issue of infertility, you can probably point to a time in your life when you wondered if God had forgotten you.

Imagine you were in Abram or Sarai's place. Ten years had passed since God's promise that your descendants would become a great nation, in Genesis 12:2. For many years, God had been silent regarding how and when His covenant with you would be fulfilled. Suddenly, God appears to you (see Genesis 15:1–6) and you find yourself standing outside, gazing at the night sky unobstructed by today's city glare as the Lord compares your future and immeasurable offspring with the innumerable stars of the sky. As with many other characters in the Bible, and probably with us today, clarity came only in hindsight for Abram and Sarai. In the midst of those years of silence, even a man of great faith such as Abram struggled with God's way and timing. He even struggled with the lack of God's presence! He worried. He looked elsewhere for answers.

Abram was looking for answers to his uncertainties, but the Lord wanted him to look up. God's dynamic and starry sermon illustration provided a vision for what He planned to do through Abram's example of trust and obedience. Yet when God finally spoke, with this promise beautifully illustrated by the stars in the heavens, Abram "*believed in the Lord*" (Genesis 15:6). Here we see that even after ten years of God's silence, and having absolutely nothing to show for it, Abram cast himself on the unfailing *chesed* (Hebrew word translated most often as "lovingkindness" or "grace") love of God. Abram trusted in God's covenant faithfulness and he decided, against all odds, to trust in God's character. Abram affirmed his trust in God's covenant faithfulness and was declared righteous. His faith (*'ā·măn*)—which in Hebrew means "to be convinced, have confidence, to trust," very similar to our English *amen*[4]—is cited again and again in the New Testament as the doctrine of imputed righteousness. (See, for instance, Romans 4:3, 9, 33; Galatians 3:6; James 2:23.)

Fast-forward to Genesis 17, Abram is now ninety-nine years old (he was seventy-five when God initially promised his progeny), twenty-four years after promising Abram a son, and thirteen years after confirming His covenant. God changes Abram's name to Abraham ("father of multitudes"). Therefore, Abraham's transformation occurred in the midst of God's silence, because he had cast himself unreservedly on the character of *El Shaddai*—God Almighty. (Genesis 17:1, "*When Abram was ninety-nine years old the* Lord *appeared to Abram and said to him, 'I am* ***God Almighty.'***") Thankfully the story does not end there. When we study the narratives of the Bible, we must remember that these are not fairy tales. These characters in the Bible are not super heroes or robots. They were normal people, like you and me. One of the most relevant and rewarding aspects of studying the Bible is that the central characters and narratives are so approachable. We can read our stories into the biblical epic as though we were present, watching the scenes as they unfolded, taking hold of timeless principles and examples of faith. What would your response be to God after twenty-four years of silence? After sixteen verses of God proclaiming His might and power (see Genesis 17:1–16), Abraham responds in a most human way: he laughed in God's face. Abraham's name has been changed yet his immediate reaction was to laugh at God (see Genesis 17:17–18), which was an expression of disbelief and doubt.

Guess what? God has a sense of humor, too. God said in Genesis 17:19 that Abraham shall name his son Isaac ("laughter") so that each time Abraham calls for his son, he will always be reminded that God transcended his momentary doubts and kept His covenant promise. No wonder God asked a third person a question of Himself: "*Is anything too hard for the* Lord*?*" (Genesis 18:14). Perhaps you have laughed in disbelief at God's apparent absence in your life. It may be that you identify with the father in Mark 9, a believer who struggled with a chronically-ill son, who said to Jesus, "*I believe; help my unbelief!*" (Mark 9:24). In this case, Jesus did not berate the father for his believing unbelief! Jesus healed his child and we learn a dynamic lesson: some of the most faithful believers struggle with moments of intense doubt as a result of the adversities in life.

Not only is God's silence real, biblical and personal, it is also common. Consider Joseph's experience with the silence of God. Joseph was obedient to God; he trusted, obeyed, followed, and ended up in a foreign land, Egypt, a teenage victim, sold in a human trafficking transaction (see Genesis 37:1–36) to become a slave in Potiphar's house. Joseph was wrongly accused and Potiphar had Joseph thrown in an Egyptian prison. (See Genesis 39:1–23.) Many overlook the description in Psalm 105:17–19: "*...Joseph, who was sold as a slave. They hurt his feet with shackles; his* *neck was put in an iron collar. Until the time his prediction came true, the word of the* LORD *tested him*" (HCSB).

Genesis 40 concludes by saying Joseph was forgotten in prison. God's silence. The meta-narrative was that God did not want Joseph to remain in the land of Canaan, where his family would have most likely died from famine. God did not want Joseph as a slave in Potipher's house, either. God wanted Joseph to be Pharaoh's prisoner. Why? Because God wanted to favor him in the eyes of Pharaoh. God's silence was a test. Joseph's transformation to becoming the second-most powerful man in Egypt happened through God's silence.

Therefore, God's silence can lead to our transformation.

The faithful Old Testament prophets Isaiah, Jeremiah, Daniel, and Ezekiel all experienced God's silence. God's silence is biblical, personal, common, and ***not always a bad thing.***

So here is the key application: when the silence is real in your life you must recognize that you are not alone in the stillness. In fact, you are in good company. A right biblical framework will cause you to think rightly about your experiences. What is it about human nature that we constantly doubt ourselves? When you realize that Abraham, Joseph, and many of the great prophets all persevered and were eventually promoted through God's silence, we remember we are not alone. First Peter 4:12–13 says, "*Dear friends, don't be surprised when the fiery ordeal comes among you to test you as if something unusual were happening to you. Instead, rejoice as you share in the sufferings of the Messiah, so that you may also rejoice with great joy at the revelation of His glory*" (HCSB).

God was not done teaching Audrey or me what to do in His silence. These stories remind us that when we cannot see the hand of God, we must trust in His heart and character. When I fail to understand why things are going the way they are in my life, I must remember that God sees the end from the beginning and He wants me to trust Him, just like Abram and Sarai. Once we understood the relevance of God's silence, He was ready to reveal three more vital principles, as we encountered our Savior in the silence. To those important points we now turn.

3

ANTICIPATING THE SAVIOR IN THE SILENCE

There are thousands of promises in the Bible. Does this mean believers are exempt from trials, tribulations, and pain? Do the promises in the Bible guarantee the child of God a problem-free, worry-free existence? Unfortunately, the message we hear from so many "Christian" teachers in the media is not the same message found in Scripture; namely, when you walk with God your life will always be blessed, exempt from trouble. I have learned much from other believers traveling in China and Palestine. One Chinese missionary said to me, "Everything you read about in the book of Acts is happening in China right now!" That is a bold statement and yet, when you come face-to-face with Chinese believers, you are immediately drawn to their passion for Christ and willingness to suffer for His name. Miracles are occurring with regularity in China. God is active in His church. The Chinese church expects persecution. Like Paul, the Chinese church rejoices in her suffering.

The believers we encountered in the West Bank in Israel are certainly regarded as outcast—being Palestinian and Christian. Their fellow Palestinian Muslims regularly vandalize the church grounds, set fire to the church lawn, and threaten the leadership and attenders. I will never forget what the local pastor in Bethlehem said to me: "Dr. Johnston, our church members would never understand much of the Christian theology in the West, a theology that says coming to Christ will bless your life with ease and comfort." His remarks were striking. The believers we visited in China, the West Bank, and other "closed" countries understand and appropriate the words of Paul in 1 Corinthians 15:31: "*I* [face death] *every day!*" Persecuted Christians have met God—*in His silence and their persecution*—and are multiplying.

As we discovered in chapter 2, answering the nagging unanswered question of God's silence, divine silence is biblical, personal, common, and not always a bad thing. In fact, some of the most important Bible figures experienced years of God's silence, which He used for their ultimate transformation. It is encouraging to know that a follower of Jesus is not perfect, only forgiven. Authenticity was on display when Abraham, after a quarter century of God's silence, and at the ripe old age of ninety-nine, laughed in God's face at the promise of a child, let alone a new nation of descendants. This first principle can be learned, in a careful study of Scripture, quite apart from experiencing the silence of God in one's own life. However, the following three principles cannot be learned until they are experienced, as Audrey and I discovered, journaling through five years of heavenly silence. The silence of God is a deeply personal issue experienced by scores of Christians in churches around the world. With so little written on the subject of God's apparent silence, and still fewer sermons where it is referenced, we were forced into the uncharted, foggy waters of total dependence on a God whom, we thought, might have abandoned us. As it turns out, that is right were we need to be.

The Silence of God Should Always Lead to the Psalms

Did you know that Jesus of Nazareth quoted from the Psalms more than any other Old Testament book? As a Gospels scholar dedicating my life to the study of the historical Jesus, I saw this point as a ray of hope in an otherwise dreary stretch of God's hiddenness. One Bible scholar claimed that nearly all the 2,461 verses comprising the 150 chapters of the Psalms is a promise from God.[5] Certainly, no other book of the Bible is studied, memorized, quoted, prayed through, sung, or appealed to more than the Psalms, but why, as it relates to the silence of God?

Have you thought about Jesus' excruciating experience of the silence and utter abandonment of God the Father? In His native Aramaic tongue we hear Jesus' struggle: *"And at the ninth hour Jesus cried with a loud voice, 'Eloi, Eloi, lema sabachthani?' which means 'My God, my God, why have you forsaken me?'"* (Mark 15:34, see also Matthew 27:46; Luke 23:46).

In a way that we cannot humanly, theologically, or spiritually comprehend, there was silence with the Triune Godhead so much so that Jesus asked His Father, in effect, "Where are You?" Jesus was suffering such intense torment that He was almost beyond recognition—see for example, Isaiah 52:14 (HCSB): *"His appearance was so disfigured that He did not look like a man, and His form did not resemble a human being"*—yet His deepest agony was the experience of God's silence. It is here that the principle emerges. The apex of Jesus' sense of God's silence, from memory, He cried out, appealing to the Psalms, and quoted a messianic psalm of King David struggling with God's silence:

My God, my God, why have you forsaken me?
Why are you so far from saving me,
so far from my cries of anguish?
My God, I cry out by day, but you do not answer,
by night, but I find no rest.

(Psalm 22:1–2 NIV)

In Luke's narrative we learn that in spite of God's silence, Jesus placed His confidence in His Father's character: *"Father, into your hands I commit my spirit!*" (Luke 23:46). It is helpful to imagine the silence at the tomb of Jesus; yet through that silence, the greatest miracle in human history occurred: Jesus was bodily resurrected! Death was defeated. From Jesus' example, I learned in my own life that when I am agonizing with God's silence (i.e. "Father, where are You?"), I, like Jesus, will put my mind and heart in the Psalms.

The Psalms are rich with the transparency of believers who struggle with God's silence, question His plan, bemoan unanswered questions, but ultimately cast themselves on His faithful love and character. Psalm 44, in its entirety, is a tapestry of the silence of God that concludes with a triumphant note of trusting the unfailing love of God: "*We are brought down to the dust; our bodies cling to the ground. Rise up and help us; reduce us because of your unfailing* [in Hebrew: *chesed*] *love*" (verses 25–26 NIV). Psalm 62, another psalm of David, begins "*For God alone my soul waits in silence; from Him comes my salvation*" (verse 1 AMP), and after extolling God's righteous *I-never-break-my-promises* character, David exclaims "*trust in Him at all times*" (Psalm 62:8 NASB). The silence of God drives us to dependence and trust in God's unfailing (*chesed*) love, in which we ultimately discover our transformation. Before we can help others who struggle with this question of "What do I do when God is silent?" we must come to terms with this question personally. Once you understand what Scripture says about His silence (yes, that's a paradoxical statement!), you can allow God's Word to overflow from you as you talk with others.

The silence of God drove Audrey and me to the Psalms and at the intersection of the Psalms and silence, we met Jesus in all of His glory and humanity. We followed our Savior's example, He memorized the Psalms, which were in His heart and on His lips during his greatest torment. In our study of the psalms of David (comprising at least 73 of the 150 chapters), we were arrested by the forty verses of Psalm 37, which I believe contains a promise is each verse. My wife led by example in committing three passages in particular to memory, which would be a serviceable road reminding us of God's faithfulness through the uncharted path of His silence:

Trust in the LORD, *and do good;*
dwell in the land, and befriend faithfulness.

Delight yourself in the Lord,
  and he will give you the desires of your heart.
Commit your way to the Lord,
  trust in him, and he will act.

(Psalm 37:3–5)

The Silence of God Leads to Stones of Remembrance

One of the most debilitating results of the Fall (see Genesis 3) is forgetfulness. We need constant reminders. Our minds are careless, often distracted, inattentive to the things of God, and unmindful when He is speaking. Have you ever noticed how forgetful we all can be? There is a reason we have memorials in our nation's capital. We must be reminded of significant events of our past. As God deepens your spiritual life and molds you on the Potter's wheel of His silence, I encourage to journal as a reminder, a memorial, if you will, not only of His deliverance in your life but also of the eternal lessons learned.

In Joshua 4, Joshua crossed the Jordan River in flood season on dry ground to begin the conquest of the land promised to Abraham. As this miracle unfolded Joshua designated one person each from the twelve tribes to take up stones from the middle of the Jordan river to erect at their encampment at Gilgal (roughly a mile from Jericho): "*When your children ask in time to come, 'What do those stones mean to you?' then you shall tell them that the waters of the Jordan were cut off before the ark of the covenant of the* Lord. *When it passed over the Jordan, the waters of the Jordan were cut off. So these stones shall be to the people of Israel a memorial forever*" (Joshua 4:6–7).

We have memorial stones in our lives today, too. What about your memorial stones? Moments when God protected you; moments when God provided miraculously; moments when God divinely led you. We are directed to remember these memorial stones in times of adversity (and in silence). What did you learn in those moments? What primacy did God give you? In what way did He protect you? What wrong theology or worldly skin did you shed as God grew you in the silence?

Often times God does not answer a specific prayer, because He knows better than we do what is best for us. I recall some specific prayer requests in my life that I once passionately laid at the throne of grace, and now, in hindsight, I am so grateful that God did not answer some of those prayers! God blessed me with His silence to those petitions because He had an answer that was far better for me, but even more important, better for His glory. Here is a key principle to hold on to: God sometimes says "no" to a good request because He has the best for us.

Oswald Chambers put it this way:

> Some prayers are followed by silence because they are wrong, others because they are bigger than we can understand. It will be a wonderful moment for some of us when we stand before God and find that the prayers we clamored for in early days and imagined were never answered, have been answered in the most amazing way, and that God's silence has been the sign of the answer.[6]

Or perhaps more striking, William Culbertson, the post-World War II president of Moody Bible Institute, once remarked, "Keep praying, but be thankful that God's answers are wiser than your prayers!"[7] We generally see our lives from a limited point of view. Remember that God has an eternal perspective on everything that happens, not only in His creation but also in our personal lives.

The Silence of God Can Lead Us from Transformation to Triumph

In the midst of the 2007–2008 financial collapse I was serving on a pastoral staff that was led of God to pray over our congregation, many of whom were experiencing layoffs, uncertainty, and unexplained health crises. One Sunday in particular, a faithful family in our church, originally from India, came forward at the end of a service and specifically asked that I might pray over them to become pregnant. They had been struggling with infertility for months and, in the spirit of James 5:14, they asked me to pray over them and anoint them with oil. Can you imagine how ill-equipped I felt to pray over this couple struggling with the very issue that my wife I had been struggling with for years? I have to be honest, I almost passed on this request. Nonetheless, I dutifully and feebly prayed over this fine Christian couple, anointing them with oil and asking God to give them a child. Evidently God was testing me, because less than a year later I was overjoyed to receive their birth announcement in the mail! In my journal, I wrote that apparently my prayers for conceiving children were efficacious for others but not for my own wife. It was a test from God and an issue of trust.

The final principle Audrey and I distilled in our experience of God's silence was that He not only wanted to transform us, He also desired to lead us to triumph. Persevering through the testing of God's silence brought abundant deepening and transformation in our marriage, our personal lives, and our walk with Christ, but that was only the comma, not the full stop. We persevere in the silence of God because He wants to promote us.

In 2 Kings 20 and 2 Chronicles 32, we learn that God specifically tested King Hezekiah: "*God left* [Hezekiah] *to himself, in order to test him and to know all that was in his heart*" (2 Chronicles 32:31). Hezekiah, as Solomon before him, was a marvelous leader, visionary, and builder, yet God "*left him*" for a period of time to test his pride. In God's absence, would Hezekiah still seek the Lord? Or would he try to stand in his own strength? Perhaps you have experienced success and victories, but now it seems that God is testing you in order to discover "all that is in your heart."

Though it is certainly not always the case, we learn from the Scriptures that God tests us with His silence, often because we have allowed disobedience in our lives. Following a lifetime of disobedience we read that God left Samson in perhaps the most cryptic verse in the Bible: "*But* [Samson] *did not know that the LORD had left him*" (Judges 16:20). God was also silent to King Saul because of sustained sin. A comparison of King Saul with King David reveals an important case study in the proper and improper responses to God's silence.

In 1 Samuel 15, Samuel told Saul that God had rejected him as king of Israel because of his partial obedience, which, in God's eyes, equated to total disobedience: "*For you have rejected the word of the LORD, and the LORD has rejected you from being the king over Israel"* (1 Samuel 15:26). If you desire to know how *not* to respond to God's silence, study 1 Samuel 15–31 and you will watch Saul descend to the point of doing the unthinkable. Cut off from God, drowning in God's silence, 1 Samuel 28:6 states, *"And when Saul inquired of the LORD, the LORD did not answer him."* Facing the silence of God, Saul did the unimaginable: He visited the witch of Endor, behind enemy lines in Philistine territory, to seek guidance for victory in battle. After eliminating nearly all the mediums from Israel, King Saul put on a disguise and visited a necromancer. (See 1 Samuel 28:7–20.) In retelling the story, the chronicler explicitly states that Saul died from consulting the dead rather than consulting God. (See 1 Chronicles 10:13–14.) Saul was defeated in battle and completed suicide on Mount Gilboa, and the Philistines mounted his body in Beth-Shan for all to see. (See 1 Samuel 31.) There is an important parallel between Saul and David.

In 1 Samuel 16, David was anointed king of Israel after God rejected Saul; however, according to the chronology, David was not crowned king for an additional fifteen years. In fact, after being promised the kingdom, David was regularly hunted by Saul, who sought to take his life. In 1 Samuel 30, while David was on a mission fighting the Philistines, the Amalekites descended on David's encampment and captured all his wives and children, as well as his mighty men. How did David respond to this disappointment after defeat? How did David respond to the juxtaposition of God's promise to be king and His fifteen-year silence? David's response is best viewed through the lens of 1 Samuel 30:6, in view of all this disappointment and God's responding silence: *"David was greatly distressed.... But David strengthened himself in the LORD his God."* Unlike Saul, David would not stop persevering in God's silence, and continued to seek Him, no matter the outcome. Whereas Saul responded by seeking a medium, David sought the face of God Almighty. Eventually, God rescued the wives and children of David and his mighty men and after fifteen years of silence, David was finally anointed king of Israel.

Where do you find yourself in these stories? The lesson is that for us to reach our destiny, we must go through the testing of silence, like Hezekiah, David, Abraham, Sarah, Joseph, Hannah, and even Jesus. Will you commit to respond to God in His silence by continuing to seek Him? Will you cast yourself on the unfailing love of God? More than two hundred fifty times in the Old Testament we read of the *chesed*—the unfailing—loving-kindness, eternal love of God. His *chesed* love for us is unfailing because He cannot fail, and therefore, His love for us will triumph in our lives.

4

BEING A CHANNEL, NOT A RESERVOIR: UNANSWERED ENGAGEMENT PRINCIPLES

I needed better answers. After receiving thousands of questions from seekers, skeptics, and Jesus followers at Christian Thinkers Society, we realized that to be effective in our ministry we needed to make certain we understood what the real questions were in the church today. As we aggregated all of the questions we received, we realized that there was a significant divide between the topics normally discussed in the pulpit and the actual unanswered grass root questions that existed in our congregations. The stakes were high. Therefore, we needed better answers, but not only answers at the intellectual level, we also needed answers that would inspire spiritual engagement. The most significant asset in the church today is its people. Unfortunately, we have not fully maximized the potential of our church members. Our current version of Christianity has been dumbed down in so many respects and contexts that it has become inert.

What troubles me is that in the whole history of the church, the twenty-first century has some of the most educated people ever sitting in its pews, yet they are also the most unengaged and biblically illiterate. It is not only ignorance of the Bible that concerns me; it is also the frequent misrepresentation of the Bible's message. Today's increasingly anti-Christian climate constantly distorts, twists, and takes the Bible out of context. The results of this massive non-engagement by the majority of Christians is stark. Missiologists predict that, by 2025, only 15 percent of Americans will attend church with any type of regularity.[8]

Notwithstanding this prediction, I have never been more encouraged than I am today in considering the unrealized potential of the church, especially with my fellow millennials. In scores of churches across multiple denominations, I have seen a growing hunger for God's Word, among young and old Christians alike. Many of them are weary of the modern Christian message coming across as unthinkingly weak, when there are robust answers to life's deepest unanswered questions found within our faith. The mission of *Unanswered* is for you to become resourced; namely, receiving answers to your own unanswered questions, but also empowered to engage the content of these answers in order to bring freedom in your own community.

Knowledge without action is useless, and unfortunately, there is a myriad of intellectually useless Christians in the church. They think they might have all of the answers, but when is the last time they actually had a meaningful faith dialogue? We can do better. I have encountered numerous Christians who know much of the Bible and are completely useless when it comes to engagement. If the gospel is going to spread it will require ordinary men and women to be informed about their faith and confident to engage the unanswered questions of our time.

In his biography of C. S. Lewis, Alister McGrath aptly described the attraction and sustaining power of Christianity as its ability to answer the questions of a world that confronts our faith: "[we are in] the business of identifying, understanding, and answering concerns and difficulties that ordinary people have about the Christian faith, and also demonstrating its power to explain things and satisfy the deepest longings of the human heart."[9] Having witnessed the life-changing power in an answered question, especially as it relates to the six specific questions addressed in this book, the final chapter in each of the six sections of this book will focus on implementing these important answers with five essential *Unanswered Engagement Principles*:

Don't Go Beast-Mode. The principle of learning to answer tough questions in a winsome way as a thoughtful ambassador of Christ. (Chapter 7)

Shut Up and Listen! Leaders are great listeners. The principle of learning to listen to what the questions actually are rather than deploying a shock-and-awe argument for the Christian faith. (Chapter 10)

Be Cool, Thought Leader. The more we know and understand our faith, the more "chillaxed" we will be responding to questions about it. (Chapter 13)

Be Curious. The art of asking the right questions while allowing the other person to be an "expert." Being smart about your personal faith does not mean you think others are stupid. (Chapter 16)

Avoid Island Fever. To engage others requires leaving the island of our personal comfort zone. Jesus was the friend "of sinners." (Chapter 19)

In conclusion, I have learned that you never say "never" in my line of work. As a biblical scholar and author, I never say that we have heard the last uncritical theory about Jesus or the historic Christian faith. Ridiculous claims and sensational attacks on Christianity seem to pop up twice a year, *ad nauseam*—right before Christmas and Easter. As a follower of Jesus, never say never and always be ready. The sad reality is that most

Christians are not equipped to answer even the most pedestrian questions about their personal faith. Almost everyone is concerned about the questions we have aggregated in *Unanswered*, but few people have the courage to voice them. Believers and numerous pastors, if they are honest, often struggle to understand and explain the salient issues of Christianity—even their *own* faith—to their closest friends. The wealth of published materials available from modern Christian apologists reveal that we have done an effective job listening to the questions of atheists, agnostics, seekers, and other self-described non-believers; however, have we listened close enough to the questions our own congregations are asking? The sad reality is that fellow believers make destructive decisions every day because of unanswered questions. Within this tension is an unprecedented opportunity for engagement.

The additional component of Engagement Principles makes this book unique, in that we are not only answering your own unanswered questions but we are also inspiring you to translate these answers to the world around you through leadership engagement. There is courage in closing in on the unanswered questions of our time with the benefit of confidence that springs within the individual who can respond in a biblically sound and culturally sensitive way. C. S. Lewis wrote, in *Christian Apologetics*, "Power to translate is the test of having really understood one's own meaning."[10] This is precisely my ambition in this book. A believer possessing the power to explain and answer tough questions about his or her faith not only meets the needs of their community, but also proves that they have understood the meaning of their own faith. In summary, one will leave this study enriched and characterized by a *thinking faith*, capable of communicating confidently, and committed to escaping the tendency to offer trite answers to a skeptical world. In completing this study, the purpose is not to become a reservoir of knowledge, but a channel of truth.

PART 2

BODY OF PROOF: WHY CAN I TRUST IN THE BODILY RESURRECTION OF JESUS AND HOW DOES THAT CHANGE THINGS TODAY?

5

THE DEAD RISE: A PH.D. IN ZOMBIES

We live in a culture fascinated and entertained by the notion of the risen dead. Zombies, "walkers," and the undead, whichever name you prefer, have never been more popular or profitable. Some of the highest-rated television shows of all time focus on dead bodies coming back to life. One example is AMC's hit series *The Walking Dead,* which habitually draws "monster" ratings, with more than fifteen million weekly viewers.[11] To put it in another light, more Americans watch *The Walking Dead* than the World Series[12] or NBA Finals.[13] The dead are not only rising in entertainment circles, but in scholarship as well. *The Wall Street Journal* recently reported that it is now possible to earn a Ph.D. in zombie studies at American universities, such as the University of Arizona.[14] An important comparison is essential in considering our modern mind-set toward the undead and our mind-set toward bodily resurrection in the first-century world of Jesus. To the modern mind the dead rising is intriguing, even entertaining; however, in the New Testament world, the idea of bodily resurrection was unheard of in Roman circles. With the exception of Judaism and nascent Christianity, no Roman believed in resurrection. In fact, the Romans viewed resurrection as a gross and disgusting concept.[15]

The Resurrection of Jesus: A Ghost Story?

Why do we celebrate Easter rather than Halloween as a cardinal Christian day of celebration? After all, belief in ghosts was widespread among Romans, and even Jews, in the first century. Ghost stories were much more acceptable in Judaica and the wider Mediterranean world than the thought of a corporeal body returning from the dead. In the first century, ghosts were feared and demons were thought of as the wicked dead, able to bring pain and suffering on the living, as Jospheus and Philo attest (*J.W.* 7.185, *Embassy to Gaius* 65).[16] Improper or unceremonious burial was believed to enjoin the wicked spirits of the departed to haunt and even kill.[17] Similar to more modern vampire tales, the only certain way to ensure that the dead did not return as vindictive ghosts was incineration.[18] For example, most likely fearing demonic, ghostly retribution, Emperor Caligula, who was savagely assassinated in AD 41 (see Seutonius, *Caligula* 58.3), was cremated. Suetonius states:

> His body was conveyed secretly to the gardens of the Lamian family, where it was partly consumed on a hastily erected pyre and buried beneath a light covering of turf; later his sisters on their return from exile dug it up, cremated it, and consigned it to the tomb. Before this was done, it is well known that the caretakers of the gardens were disturbed by ghosts, and that in the house where he was slain not a night passed without some fearsome apparition, until at last the house itself was destroyed by fire. (*Caligula* 59)[19]

In Matthew 14:22–33, Jesus' disciples were terrified when they witnessed Him walking on the Sea of Galilee and imagined they saw a ghost: *"But when the disciples saw him walking on the sea, they were terrified, and said, 'It is a ghost!' and they cried out in fear"* (verse 26, see also Mark 6:49). In describing the disciple's fear the Greek word *phantasma* is used, from which we derive our English word *phantom* or *ghost*. In His Sunday evening resurrection appearance to the eleven gathered in Jerusalem (see Luke 24:36–49), Jesus had to convince the disciples that He was not an apparition: *"See my hands and my feet, that it is I myself. Touch me, and see. For a spirit does not have flesh and bones as you see that I have"* (Luke 24:39). Perhaps my favorite resurrection saying attributed to Jesus is *"Have you anything here to eat?"* (verse 41), because of the type of postmortem appearance it entails. Jesus then proceeded to dine on a piece of broiled fish (apparently He was not a vegetarian). Imagine the Eleven watching their resurrected Lord slowly eat His dinner before their very eyes, knowing that only days before, He had been slaughtered by the Roman occupiers. This resurrected Jesus was no ghost or apparition by virtue of the fact that in tales of ghosts, they generally do not eat. Therefore, what happened at Easter overwhelmed the followers of Jesus to such an extent that it dominated their thoughts and became the very center of their preaching.

A key point to consider is that the early church could not have selected a more difficult talking point to launch their new movement than by proclaiming to the Mediterranean world that their Savior, a convicted and executed criminal of Rome, had in fact risen from the dead. The only reason the early Christian movement taught and eventually died proclaiming a bodily resurrection was because it actually happened.

The heart of the Christian message is the bodily resurrection of Jesus of Nazareth. Even so, the claim that Jesus was truly resurrected assumed a heavy burden of proof. Why did Jesus' followers think that He had been resurrected? What persuaded them? It would have been much easier, and certainly more culturally palatable, to proclaim that Jesus was a ghostly apparition. In his Pentecost sermon Peter proclaimed, *"This Jesus God raised up, and of that we* ***all*** *are witnesses"* (Acts 2:32). It is noteworthy that Peter pointed out that they *"all"* were witnesses. This testimony of a bodily resurrection, not a ghostly apparition, was not a rumor. It was not vague, third-hand hearsay, rather it was known by eyewitnesses and seen by *"all."* Who could dispute it? Where were the voices of the objectors? The resurrected Jesus was seen and experienced by Jesus' own disciples and dozens of others. Notice it was the women who observed the place where Jesus was buried. (See Mark 15:47.) All four gospel writers report that it was women—the same women who supported Jesus during His earthly ministry (see Luke 8)—who first witnessed the empty tomb. The Lukan tradition portrays at least five women—two Marys and Joanna—and adds *"the other women"* (Luke 24:10) without any more specificity.

Among the better-known objectors of the risen Lord were Celsus and Porphyry, philosophers who ridiculed the Christian proclamation of the resurrection of Jesus on the basis that it rested upon little more than the confused and contradictory testimony of frightened women.[20] Celsus (writing sometime in AD 175–181), Porphry (AD 234–303), and other early objectors were quick to judge the early Christian movement for resting their case for Jesus' bodily resurrection with female witnesses: "But who really saw [the resurrection]? A hysterical woman...."[21] We have to be careful not to read our modern understanding back into the Bible, though many do and unwittingly distort its meaning. In the first-century world, a woman would have been an embarrassing first witness of such a monumental event. Women were not viewed as reliable sources. Jews and Pagans alike scoffed at this proclamation, especially in the second century.

Furthermore, what persuaded Jesus' followers to speak of resurrection was their conviction that Jesus had died, was buried in a known place, and had left that tomb.[22] Jesus was not only seen after the resurrection, being physically present, but His disciples were able to reach out and touch Him; indeed, He had an appetite and sat down to eat. Many miss the important detail revealed in John's gospel, *"Simon Peter...entered the tomb; and he saw the linen wrappings lying there"* (John 20:6 NASB). This evidential thread suggests that Jesus' body was not merely moved or stolen, because it would have been unnecessary to unwrap His corpse. The grave clothes were left behind. Jesus was not there. It was the combination of these factors—both the empty tomb and the multiple attested appearances of Jesus—that convinced His followers that God had acted decisively in Jesus Christ—in His incarnation, death, and resurrection—who is sufficient to bring salvation to everyone who embraces the gospel. The resurrection threw Jesus' entire message of the kingdom of God into a new light.

The resurrection of Jesus Christ is the seminal issue for the church today, as it was that first Easter morning in Jerusalem. If the resurrection did not happen, Christianity is a waste of time. If I were a critic of Christianity, perhaps the most difficult problem would be coming up with a reason for why there are any Christians (*Christianoi*) in the first place. Their founder was a crucified criminal. Crucifixion was considered to be the most heinous and shameful way to die. In the gospel of Luke, His disciples are said to have lost all hope following the crucifixion. They gave up, and why would they not? In that gripping scene in Luke 24:13–35, two disciples on the Emmaus road encounter an interesting stranger. Not realizing they are walking and conversing with the resurrected Messiah, they admitted, *"we had hoped that he was the one"* (Luke 24:21), with a particular note of defeat. The early Christian movement should have died out, but instead it thrived. Why? *The resurrection of Jesus.*

No greater words were ever uttered than when Jesus promised, *"because I live, you also will live"* (John 14:19). These words should influence every aspect of our lives. There are approximately 138,000 words in the composite Greek New Testament. Paul wrote thirteen of the twenty-seven New Testament books and contributed an approximate total of 32,407 words, or nearly 25 percent of the Bible. Of course, only "Dr. Luke," with his Luke/Acts series, contributed more to the New Testament corpus than Paul. Do you recall what the apostle Paul said was the most essential topic in all of his important writings? In 1 Corinthians 15:3 Paul makes clear what is at stake by asserting the issue of Jesus' bodily resurrection was a matter *"of first importance"*—*protois* in the Greek, meaning first. The bodily resurrection of Jesus was the pivot point of the new faith.

Recovering a Resurrection-Centric Faith

The early Christian movement influenced most of the Roman Empire in a rather short of period of time. Belief in the bodily resurrection of Jesus was the driving force behind the growth and expansion of the early church from one hundred twenty people in the upper room to a movement that, by the time it had reached Thessalonica in Greece, had *"turned the world upside down"* (Acts 17:6).

Every sermon recorded in Acts discusses the resurrection of Jesus. The book of Romans is regarded as the most important piece of literature in history and is often referenced as the most significant book ever written. We are on the eve of the five hundredth anniversary of Martin Luther and his spiritual awakening. Luther's study of Romans led to a reformation not only in his life but also throughout much of the church. (See chapter 14 for more on Martin Luther.) In the opening verses of Romans, Paul gloriously states that Jesus *"was declared to be the Son of God in power...by his resurrection from the dead"* (Romans 1:4). To the Philippians Paul said, *"I want you to know Christ and the experience the mighty power that raised him from the dead"* (Philippians 3:10 NLT). More than two dozen times in the New Testament, followers of Jesus are promised they will be raised with Jesus. No other promise occurs with more frequency than the assurances of the believer's resurrection, because it is linked with Jesus' personal resurrection. (See Romans 6:4; 8:11; Ephesians 2:6.)

The early Christian message had a potency and relevance; it was not exclusive but inclusive and accepting of all classes, no matter one's social demographic. The early church was resurrection-centric in all its teaching and mission. We have missed this important point in modern Christendom. Think about it for a moment: How many sermons have you heard in the last year on the subject of the bodily resurrection of Jesus? When I speak in churches and ask this question, the most frequent reply is: (a) most cannot remember the last sermon they heard on the resurrection of Jesus, or (b) outside of Easter Sunday or the occasional funeral, the resurrection is rarely referenced. This is also true among some of our best and brightest Christian students. I regularly teach Masters courses to Christianity majors and many of them get a deer-in-the-headlights look in their eyes when asked for the evidential basis for why they believe a dead Man returned to life two thousand years ago. As followers of Jesus, all of us—not a select few professors or popular Christian authors—have to prepare ourselves, as the early church did, to persuasively explain why Jesus' resurrection is not a myth, legend, or fairytale, but rather a datum of historical fact.

One newspaper recently caught my attention with an article "Easter Sunday is the Super Bowl of Church Attendance," noting that more people attend church on Easter Sunday than watch the Super Bowl.[23] Many respect the resurrection yet few Christians are able to offer a compelling answer for how they *know* Jesus rose from the grave. Many believers have never gone deeper than their elementary Sunday school learning when it comes to the principle points of our faith. It is time to own it. *You need to own your faith.* When God gives you an opportunity to speak up for the resurrection of Jesus, be it in a plane seat or a classroom, you need to own the situation. The church needs a fresh commitment to spending more time teaching and extolling this matter *"of first importance."*[24]

The church is, and should be, resurrection-centric because the bodily resurrection of Jesus guarantees our future resurrection; they are linked: *"If the Spirit of him who raised Jesus from the dead dwells in you, he who raised Christ Jesus from the dead will also give life to your mortal bodies"* (Romans 8:11). Only because of the resurrection could Paul say to the Colossian church, *"Christ in you, the hope of glory"* (Colossians 1:27). Do you possess a resurrection-centric faith? If you were asked to unpack why you believe in the resurrection of Jesus, what would you say?

Paul Sangster wrote a beautiful memoir of his father, the prominent World War II British minister by the name of Dr. William Sangster, which was released two years after his death in 1962. *Doctor Sangster* is a favorite book in my library because it reminds me of the importance of a resurrection-centric faith and how this central belief should motivate me to serve and influence the world around me now. Sangster was a man driven by his belief in resurrection as "now and not yet," which motivated him to make today was full of brighter living in the light of the resurrection.

William Sangster pastored in London for sixteen years, across the street from Westminster Abbey, at the Methodist church, The Westminster Central Hall. Five of those sixteen years were during the Nazi blitz. History tells us that during the Nazi blitz of London a conservative estimate is that sixty thousand civilians were killed. Hitler's aim was to bring Britain to submission through bombing civilian targets, an act of *total war* designed to break the heart of the country. Voices throughout England began to emerge, calling for renewed hope and strength against all odds.

On his first Sunday in 1939, the very first announcement Sangster made to his new congregation was: "My dear friends, I regret that my first announcement to you has to be that a state of war exist between this country and Germany."[25] In a matter of months, Sangster's preaching was so powerful that his church grew from three hundred on Sunday to more than three thousand regular attenders.

Remarkably, Sangster had a red warning light installed on his pulpit, because when the Nazi bombs would begin falling the light would immediately start flashing. Sangster affectionately referred to those services as "siren services."[26] Can you imagine attending church during Nazi air raids on your city? The need was so great and the hunger to hear from God was so prevalent that, despite the flashing pulpit light warning of imminent danger, thousands continued to attend the Central Hall.

Though Pastor Sangster was so busy in the work of the Lord, preaching, writing, visiting, and traveling, he began to notice unyielding pain in his throat and a delayed dragging sensation in his leg. He later learned from his physician that he had an incurable disease that caused a progressive muscular atrophy.[27] His thundering preaching voice would eventually be silenced and his throat would soon degenerate to the point of being unable to swallow. Externally he faced not only Nazi air raids, but also, internally, an incurable disease. Sangster continued steadfastly in his ministry in the church and bomb shelters, concluding that his disease would give him more time alone with the Lord.[28] Nearly a half million Londoners stayed in his church's bomb shelter over a five year period.[29] The Hall was not only Sangster's church, it was also his home, as he and his family slept in a gentleman's lavatory on the ground floor of the church. Though they could have, the Sangster family never returned to their own home during the five years of bombings. Thus, Sangster rose to prominence such that by 1946, his sermons and comments were regularly reported in the news. Sangster kept a journal throughout his illness. "Let me stay in the struggle, Lord," he would plead with God. "I don't mind if I can no longer be a general, but God give me a regiment to lead." "I'm only in the kindergarten of suffering," he would say to the friends who pitied his condition.

In his letter of retirement, Pastor Sangster, unable to preach and physically unwell, stated the most difficult part was that "part of my pain in not being able to preach is the knowledge that I have deeper things to say than I ever had."[30] With his personal physician monitoring him a few feet off the platform, Sangster preached on Felix and the peril of procrastination when God speaks to us.[31] Sangster never preached publically again, though his example still speaks to us today.

Gradually Sangster's body gave out. His legs had no muscle strength and became useless and his voice that was first "tight" was now gone.[32] Through an excruciating effort, Sangster was able to hold a pen, albeit shaking, and as his last Easter approached he wrote in his journal: "Much with the Lord today. He could have turned back. He went on. I shall never plumb the depth of this love."[33] On the final Easter morning of his life, only a few weeks before his death, he wrote a letter to his daughter, Margaret, who was in India: "It is terrible to wake up on Easter morning and have no voice to shout, 'He is Risen!'—but it would be still more terrible to have a voice and not want to shout, 'He is Risen!'"[34] Pastor Sangster exemplified a resurrection-centric life that not only gave him a future assurance, but also drove him to serve his present world:

> God was the harmonizing factor of his life. He was God-obsessed. All of his thoughts began and ended in God. It was as natural in him to talk about God as it was in another man to talk about his golf.[35]

Like Sangster, we should also be so resurrection-centric that we lead the way for a better world today, not idly waiting for the recreated world of tomorrow.

Conclusion

Resurrection, being the central tenant of the Christian faith, is no mere ghost story, but rather a fact of history. Even so, it assumes a heavy burden of proof. Is it possible that one morning changed the world? Could the answer to most if not all of life's problems be what occurred on a Sunday morning in April, AD 30?[36] Could it be that God's answer to the injustice in our world is *exactly* what happened in a Roman outpost over a thirty-nine-hour period at a Jewish criminal's borrowed tomb? Could it be so simple?

In a word, yes. The resurrection of Jesus Christ is the seminal issue for the church today, even as it was that first Easter morning. There is nothing more important for the Christian than Jesus' resurrection. And if it is indeed the central fact of our faith, something that elevates Christianity above all other belief systems in the world, why don't Christians know more about it? Unfortunately, the most important fact of the Christian faith is also the most misunderstood. Most followers of Jesus have a woefully inadequate understanding of Jesus' resurrection.

If the resurrection of Jesus is so important why is there so little attention to it in our modern church? This is incongruent with what we see in the life of the early Christian church. It is important to understand that in the world of Jesus and of the early church—that is, the first, second, and third centuries—belief in resurrection from the dead was mocked and attacked by thinkers throughout the Roman Empire. If the disciples deceptively desired to create or invent a new religion, they could not have selected a more confusing place to start than by imagining a story of a decomposing corpse coming back to life. Had the church invented the story of Jesus' resurrection, the idea of His ghostly appearance would have been much more palatable, not to mention acceptable in the first century.

In staking the claim of a resurrection body, the early Christian movement should have died! But it did not. *Why?* Because their founder was *physically* alive. The Greco-Roman culture of the first century did not understand why anyone would believe in a dead body coming back to life. The proclamation of the early Christian leaders—a ripe corpse coming back to life—would have been disgusting and strange to any Roman. Therefore, not only do we need to inculcate a renewed perspective with a resurrection-centric faith, but we also must refresh our minds with the evidence that undergirds the historical backbone for our claim that Jesus was bodily resurrected. To some of this important evidence, which buttresses the claim that Jesus was resurrected, we now turn.

6

EVIDENCE OF THE GREATEST COMEBACK EVER

Unlike any other religion, Christianity put itself to the historical test through explicit interaction with history in the Roman Empire of the first century. Many people often miss this point. No other religion comes close to Christianity in that you can test it against history! History tells us that something happened to Jesus on that early Sunday morning, which changed the lives of the people who witnessed it. (See Mark 16:14; Luke 24:34–43; John 20:19–31; Acts 1:3–4; 9:3–6 for some of these appearances.) On Friday night, the disciples were running scared. A few days later, they were more than willing to endure ridicule, imprisonment, mistreatment, and even death for what they had seen. *"As for us, we cannot help speaking about what we have seen and heard"* (Acts 4:20 NIV). I encourage you to travel back in time with me to that first Easter, an April Sunday in first-century Jerusalem.

Dating the time based on Caiaphas's removal from office as high priest, as well as the annual Jewish Passover, provides a solid evidential basis to peg the crucifixion and resurrection on Friday, April 7–9, AD 30 (April 3–5, AD 33, is an alternative date for the crucifixion of Jesus). The forecast would have called for warmer weather. The city of Jerusalem would have been brimming over with Jews who had flooded into the city for the annual Passover festival. As careful students of history we must ask how we can prove that Jesus rose from the dead. Was Jesus physically raised from the dead? How do we know for sure? What has the most explanatory power? What is the best evidence for His resurrection? Was resurrection an educated guess on the part of the New Testament authors? Did the disciples steal the body? How we answer these questions changes everything.

The Evidence for a Resurrection-Centric Faith

In chapter 5 we underscored the importance of recovering a resurrection-centric faith. While important, it is merely a launching point. We must also refresh our minds with the evidence for a resurrection-centric faith, because when we study the resurrection of Jesus—and our own eventual bodily resurrections—it brings renewal to our spiritual life. Like Pastor Sangster (see chapter 5), the truths of the resurrection give us confidence to face the tribulations and troubles of life. Christianity is quintessentially a resurrection religion. The evidence is overpowering that the main appeal to Christianity, the reason the church grew exponentially in the first few centuries, was its confident attitude toward death and expectation of a future bodily resurrection like that of their founder. From the very beginning, Christians, following Jesus' example, valued the personal survival of each individual. All life—even the lives of the elderly, young, and marginalized—all bore the *imago dei*—"the image of God." (See Genesis 1:27.) This is an essential point that modern people often miss, mainly because life expectancy levels in the West are at all-time highs. For example, life expectancy in the US averages seventy-nine years, which, according to the Center for Disease Control is the highest on record.[37] In fact, life expectancy is eight years higher today than it was in 1970.[38]

As careful Bible students we must always be wary of projecting our modern understandings into Scripture. Have you considered what the life expectancy was in the time of Jesus? I always have fun with my students in discussions related to life expectancy in the Bible. Most students suggest a life expectancy similar to our modern expectations. Hardly! Repeatedly, more than thirty times in the gospels, we are told that *"large crowds"* followed Jesus. *"Such a very large crowd gathered…that* [Jesus] *got into a boat"* (Mark 4:1 NASB) to address the crowd that had amassed by the sea. I suggest that one of the strong attractions to Jesus' ministry was the fact that life expectancy in His time was quite the opposite of today. Christianity emerged in a world of immense suffering and low life expectancy. Life expectancy in the time of Jesus and the early church averaged twenty years of age. Skeletal remains suggest that as many as one quarter (25 percent) of the Roman Empire, on any given day, was sick, dying, or in need of immediate medical attention; often only one third of the skeletons found in archeological digs from that time are those of adults. Infant mortality was as high as 30 percent; fewer than 49 percent of children saw their fifth birthday.[39] Even in the glorious city of Rome, infant mortality was common. Near the catacomb of San Panfilo, 83 of the 111 graves are of children.[40] Only 40 percent of the population lived to the age of twenty.[41] With this in mind, Jesus' reputation as a famous Miracle Worker and Healer guaranteed that people would try to touch him. (See, for instance, Mark 5:28; 6:56; 8:22; 10:13.)

The leading cause of death in the first-century Roman world of Jesus was malnutrition. Most of the empire was starving to death, and finding your next meal was always problematic for those outside of the aristocracy. Consider the effect that brevity of life had on the greater Roman society. Suddenly, there comes a Miracle Worker from Galilee, and of Him it is reported that *"the blind receive their sight, the lame walk, lepers are cleansed, and the deaf hear, the dead are raised up, the poor have the good news preached to them"* (Luke 7:22). In the light of that contextual backdrop, it is no surprise that *"a large crowd was following* [Jesus] *and pressing in on Him"* (Mark 5:24 NASB). The presence, power, and proclamation of Jesus were relevant to His first-century context in ways we hardly appreciate or imagine today. Therefore, Jesus not only discussed resurrection but He also commanded His disciples, whom He sent out as apostles, to proclaim the kingdom of God and to *"raise the dead"* (Matthew 10:8), as adumbrations of the resurrection anticipated at the end of days.[42]

Romans usually delayed the naming of their newborns for eight or nine days because, after all, a name may not be needed, especially if it was a girl. Death by exposure was common for infants. No one cared if you killed your baby, especially if the child was deformed or suffered with a handicap. Why did this custom Roman custom ultimately change? A resurrected man from Nazareth said, *"Let the children come to me…for to such belongs the kingdom of heaven"* (Matthew 19:14).

Jesus authorized His disciples to preach the good news of the reign of God and, among other things, to *"raise the dead [nekrós egeírō]."* In His reply to the imprisoned John the Baptist, Jesus said, *"the dead are raised up [nekroi egeirontai]"* (Matthew 11:5; Luke 7:22). In addition to these summary statements, the New Testament Gospels narrate three specific stories of people raised from the dead by Jesus. In one story Jesus raised the daughter of Jairus, the ruler of a synagogue, whose daughter died only moments before Jesus arrived. (See Mark 5:21–43; Matthew 9:18–26; Luke 8:40–56.) The story's details may suggest first-hand eyewitness testimony, as evidenced from the desperation of the father and the sad report that reached him, *"Your daughter is dead. Why trouble the Teacher any further?"* (Mark 5:35, see also Luke 8:49) to the mocking laughter in response to Jesus' words, *"Why are you making a commotion and weeping? The child is not dead but sleeping"* (Mark 5:39). The very Aramaic words that Jesus uttered next remain fixed in the tradition: *"'Talitha cumi,' which means, 'Little girl, I say to you, arise'"* (verse 41). The appearance of the name Jairus, along with his identification with respect to the local synagogue (probably the one at Capernaum), points to the memory of a specific episode in the ministry of Jesus.

In the second story Jesus raised up the only son of a widow. (See Luke 7:11–17.) Jesus encountered the funeral party as it left the village of Nain, on its way to the place of burial. The boy had died that very day or perhaps the previous evening. A number of distinctive details are recalled, such as the name of the village, the woman being a widow, the deceased boy, her only son, Jesus' touching of the bier, the stopping of the bearers, and the startling movement of the deceased, who is said to have *"sat up"* (verse 15). Again we have vivid details that probably derive from eyewitness memory.

The third resurrection story is the well-known raising of Lazarus, arguably the most stunning miracle story in the Jesus tradition. Lazarus was the brother of Mary and Martha, part of a family that lived in Bethany, in the vicinity of Jerusalem. (See John 11:1–44.) We are told that Lazarus had been ill, had finally died, and that four days after his death Jesus finally arrived. In contrast to the other people who had died and were raised minutes or, at most, hours later, Lazarus had been dead for four days. He had been wrapped and placed into the family tomb. The seven-day primary funeral, held at the graveside, was more than half completed. Jesus arrived, requested that the stone be removed, and was told that there would be a stench. (See verse 39.) According to Jewish tradition, the spirit of the deceased lingers in the vicinity of the corpse for three days and then departs on the fourth day. (See Lev. Rab. 18.1 [on Lev 15:1–2]; Qoh. Rab. 12:6 §1.) From the Jewish perspective of late antiquity, Lazarus was as dead as one can get. Nothing less than "resurrection," in its eschatological sense, would bring him back. His sisters believed this; but as far as this life was concerned, they never expected to see their brother again. Jesus then commanded, *"Lazarus, come out [deúro* éxō]" (John 11:43), and *"the man who had died came out, his hands and feet bound with linen strips"* (verse 44). The story is remarkable.

In all three of these stories we find what appear to be traces of eyewitness memories: the recollection of names, places, unusual and vivid details, and even some of Jesus' words. Twice we hear Him command the deceased to *"arise,"* either in Greek (see Luke 7:14) or in Aramaic (see Mark 5:41). The distinctive words of Jesus are remembered in whatever language they happen to be transmitted.

What is interesting is that in all three examples, specific details are retained: in the first story the name and position of Jairus; in the second story the name of the village and the facts that the woman was a widow and that the dead boy was her only son; and in the third story the names of the deceased and his sisters, as well as how long he had been dead and the name of their village. Clearly many details, as well as the resurrection themselves, were firmly embedded in the collective memory of Jesus' following. I emphasize these remarkable stories because it is probable that they influenced the way in which the followers of Jesus interpreted the Easter event.

From our point of view, privileged with hindsight, we may view these miraculous resuscitations as symbolic representations of the resurrection of Jesus, and of the future resurrection of His followers. But from the point of view of those who encountered the risen Jesus, men with no well-established, uniform doctrines of resurrection, the miraculous resuscitations of Jesus' ministry very probably defined aspects of His resurrection. I do not see how it could have been otherwise. Perhaps it is not coincidence that the same language used in reference to those Jesus raised up was also used in reference to His own resurrection.

Resurrection deeds were also understood to possess messianic significance. We see this in Jesus' response to John's question *"Are you the one who is to come?"* (Matthew 11:3), and in the way the Matthean evangelist introduced the exchange: *"Now when John, who was in prison, heard about the deeds of the* ***Messiah****"* (verse 2 NIV). Jesus' reply, in which He alluded to healing, raising the dead, and proclaiming goods news to the oppressed, took place with the appearance of God's Messiah. This remarkable saying (see Matthew 11:5; Luke 7:22) not only affirms Jesus' belief in resurrection but it also confirms His own messianic role in it. Consequently, the language of resurrection, not to mention deeds that Jesus and His contemporaries viewed as actual instances "being raised up" (whether resuscitation or "resurrection"), almost certainly charged the pre-Easter disciples with ideas that came into play on Easter and in the days that followed.

Christians Innovate a New Term for Burial

Have you driven by a cemetery lately? Most likely you have. Within a Greco-Roman culture that viewed resurrection belief as disgusting, the early Christian movement thrived in their resurrection-centric faith. Resurrection belief drove the Christians to value all life, which included caring for the body for burial. It is unsurprising that Christians desired to be buried together; however, they innovated a new terminology for their burial practices: the "cemetery" (*koimētērion*), because death was peacefully thought of as rest or sleep, a temporary holding place (*koimētēria* is a Greek word that refers to bedrooms, dormitories or sleeping rooms). The stratigraphy of the distinctively Christian cemetery was similar to the common Greek *necropolis,* with an added eschatological dimension associated with bodily resurrection. This is noteworthy in that early Christian burial terminology had an inherent eschatological perspective, in contrast to the wider Roman terminology for burial. For instance, a *mausoleum* for the wealthy or a *sepulcrum* as a receptacle for holding the ashes of the deceased. Perhaps the closest Latin comparison to the early Christian cemetery would be *monumentum,* which is most likely related to *moneo, monere*—"to advise or remind"—in special recognition of a life. In stark contrast to Christianity's concern for the care for the physical remains (even in burial), body dumping was a significant problem in first- and second-century Rome. It has been estimated that there were at least 1,500 abandoned corpses annually.[43] Corpses of the destitute and slaves were thrown into mass pits, or *petuculi,* where it was assumed they would be condemned to the afterlife and forgotten to eternity.[44] The fact that early Christians cared for each individual body in burial, because of a resurrection-centric faith, partially accounts for the rapid spread of the movement among the poor and slave classes in the Roman Empire.

Of course, Christianity was illegal until the fourth century (AD 313) so Christians went underground to build vast burial chambers, called *catacombs.* Perhaps you have toured the catacombs in Rome. Did you know that nearly a million Christians were interred together in Roman catacombs over the span of one hundred fifty years in the third and fourth centuries?[45]

Resurrection Belief Inspires the Earliest Christian Art

The Christian catacombs of Rome should be thought of as the first Christian art galleries. Inscriptions, symbols—such as the cross, a dove, or a fish—and creative illustrations of Christ as the Good Shepherd are some of the earliest incised Christian art. Most often the Greek word for *fish*—*ichthus*—was used as an acrostic to commemorate resurrection belief: Jesus, Christ, God, Son, Savior. When you think of the great works of Christian art, such as *The Last Supper* by Leonardo da Vinci, I hope you will remember that Christian art originated in burial grounds, known by a new term, *cemetery*, utterly influenced by the resurrection of Jesus Christ.

Matthew, Mark, Luke, and John were careful to record "*many convincing proofs*" (Acts 1:3 NIV) evidencing the bodily resurrection of Jesus. The mission of this book is to help you to complete this study with the confidence to repeat the words that Luke used to begin his gospel. After carefully investigating everything from the beginning, he wrote that it was possible for you to "*have certainty concerning the things you have been taught*" (Luke 1:4) about your Christian faith. The resurrection proves that we serve a God of second chances. Perhaps you are in need of a "do-over," a second chance in life. The resurrection promises us that God is in the business of great comebacks and new beginnings. Thanks to the veracity of the resurrection of Jesus, Christians are promised that the best is yet to come, and death is only the beginning and not the end.

As we close this chapter, I must admit that I have often seen myself among the eleven disciples, proceeding up the mount of Jesus' ascension in Matthew 28: "*When they saw him they worshiped him, but some doubted*" (verse 17). The English word *doubt* (in Greek, *distazo*) means to waiver and lack confidence in the original. Remember, these were the disciples. Where are you today on the mount of ascension? Are you worshipping or do you doubt? Notice how Jesus responded to the fact that some were worshipping while others were doubting: "*Go therefore and make disciples of all the nations, baptizing them in the name of the Father and the Son and the Holy Spirit, teaching them to observe all that I commanded you. And behold, I am with you always, to the end of the age*" (verses 19–20). Jesus put all of them to work, right where they were at, some worshipping and others doubting. Therefore, I know that I can be used by God and active in serving Him, even as I negotiate the doubts in my faith. Doubts do not sideline me. Some days I am on the mountain, seeing the resurrected Jesus and worshipping

Him; other days I find myself doubting with some of the other disciples. But God still has a plan for me, which is "Go! Be used!" The promise is clear: Jesus will be with us.

7

ENGAGEMENT PRINCIPLE #1: DON'T GO "BEAST MODE"

Going "Beast Mode" is a good thing in a full-contact sport. If you are a Seattle Seahawks fan, you most likely love the nickname "Beast Mode," which has become something of modern sports mythology. The term was coined when Seahawks running back Marshawn Lynch ripped off a stunning sixty-seven-yard touchdown romp in an upset playoff victory over the defending Super Bowl champs, the New Orleans Saints, on January 8, 2011.[46] The frenzied fans at Seattle's Qwest Field, known collectively as "the 12th man," erupted with so much noise they "triggered seismic activity near the stadium," according to the Seattle Seahawks' official website.[47] The earth shook, literally. The touchdown scamper, in which Lynch (Beast Mode) was stiff-arming defenders like they were ragdolls, has gone down in the annals of NFL history as one of the most electrifying plays of all time. Marshawn Lynch himself defined *Beast Mode,* saying, "I feel like on that field, like there is no reason why I can't run through you. I know I'm going to get got, but I'm going to get mine more than I get got though. It's really just a mindset. The Beast Mode is just something that just keeps it going."[48] The erudite *Urban Dictionary* website defines *Beast Mode* as "a hype, energetic, outgoing, wilding out state of mind."[49] The picture is becoming clearer for defining *Beast Mode*: an aggressive earthquake mind-set, with a nuanced run-you-over, out-of-my-way, frenzied energy. Unfortunately, when it comes to attempting to answer important, unanswered questions about Christianity, most Christians go into Beast Mode.

Over the years I have seen far too many scorched earth, drive-by-shooting, shout-you-down, *blitzkrieg* "evangelism" than I care to admit. Perhaps you have, too. It makes thinking people want to run for cover. This was never made clearer to me than when an individual knocked on my door and proceeded to tell me that if I did not repent I would be in hell. This person reminded me more of Beast Mode than of a compassionate Christian. I could be wrong, but my impression was that this individual appeared to want another "soul statistic" more than he wanted to express an actual concern for me. Little did he know that I am, in fact, a follower of Jesus who teaches Biblical Studies at the local university. That probably did not matter, because this guy never even bothered to ask my name. The whole conversation made me want to run away from "Beast Mode Christianity."

In another instance, I was overcome with embarrassment as I listened to a "Christian" berate a fellow airline passenger a few rows behind me. He projected a sense of superiority that would have made Darth Vader blush. The whole time I kept thinking, *You're doing it wrong!* Beast Mode Christianity.

The *New Living Bible* paraphrases Titus 2:10 by stating that all believers should *"make the teaching about God our Savior attractive* ***in every way.****"* Have you ever been in a faith conversation and a fellow Christian made a statement that was so unattractive that you wanted to disappear?

I have. Paul used the Greek word *Κοσμέω* (*kosméō*) to encourage believers to make the gospel attractive! *Kosméō* is similar to our English word *cosmetics* or *decorate*. When I take my wife on a date I get cleaned up, I put on cologne, and I attempt to look attractive for her. In a similar way, Paul says that the way we act *decorates* the gospel by making it more engaging to the world around us. So, be sure you avoid going Beast Mode!

As a teaching pastor, a local Fox News reporter, Sam, interviews me from time to time. He asks me about evidences for the Christian faith, usually around Christmas or Easter, along with a host of other questions. When our church conducted citywide outreach events and invited well-known Christian celebrities to share their faith, Sam covered the events. He listened respectfully to all of the "reasons" for the faith, but seemed indifferent. He was respectful but to him, the gospel was just another story. It turns out that Sam had weathered some terrible experiences with Beast Mode Christians in the past. What he saw in them and what he heard me say about Jesus was a striking contradiction. Sam would regale me with stories of how he lived for the weekend. He was a sharp guy—tall and blonde with a deep, resonate voice. He shared how he worked out like a maniac during the week so he could binge drink and party all weekend. Sam even won a few Emmy Awards for his reporting on breaking news.

One night I was out on a date with my wife and we were on our way home from a late movie. My phone rang and I noticed it was Sam. I was sure this was a pocket dial but I answered it anyway. "Jeremiah, this is Sam," he said. I noticed he sounded emotional, something I had never heard from him before. "I'm an alcoholic; I think I am going to kill myself tonight and I didn't know who else to call." At that moment I had a choice to make. Should I go into Beast Mode and lecture Sam on the do's and don'ts of alcohol abuse and excessive drinking? Or, should I stay on message and let him know that this Jesus, whom he knew about intellectually, was a Savior whom he could get to know experientially. I pulled to the side of the road to give my complete focus to the conversation. I walked Sam back through the love and compassion of Jesus Christ. I quoted John 3:17: *"For God did not send his Son into the world to condemn the world, but in order that the world might be saved through him."* To the glory of God, right there on that phone call, Sam trusted Jesus as his Savior and began following Him. He's sober now. He has a purpose to his life. A jaded breaking-news reporter needed to know about the compassion and forgiveness of Jesus more than a shaming manifesto from a Beast Mode Christian.

Christians need to stay on message and remain committed to the essential talking points of the gospel. Christians are not perfect, only forgiven. Your political leanings, thoughts on gun control, and views on government leaders are unnecessary and unneeded in a conversation about eternal destiny. In our post-Christian time, we must be a community of believers committed to answering the unanswered questions of life, as compassionate ambassadors of the Lord. Beast Mode is fantastic on a football field but counterproductive in a faith dialogue. Beware of going Beast Mode!

PART 3

MY INVISIBLE DISEASE: WHAT CHRISTIANS MUST UNDERSTAND ABOUT SUICIDE AND MENTAL HEALTH

8

ELEPHANT IN THE ROOM

"Wow." *Wow* is the word most often expressed when I share with friends, students, colleagues, church audiences, and publishers that the undisputed, most frequently asked questions at Christian Thinkers Society are about suicide and mental illness. For every question we receive about the Bible, we receive three questions related to suicide and other mental illnesses. For numerous reasons I believe this section of *Unanswered* is the most important resource for the unanswered questions in the church today. Because such questions are rarely voiced out loud, let alone answered, Christians fail to hear the pained and desperate whispers within our congregations. It is the "elephant in the room" of every church in North America. Suicidal thoughts and mental illness are not only common in our congregations, they have become common occurrences among pastors, as well.

While completing the final edits on this book, it saddened me to learn of yet another pastoral suicide. This time, however, it hit close to home. Only a few miles from where I was writing these paragraphs, well-known Texas pastor Phil Lineberger, 69, died by suicide on May 31, 2015. For two decades he had pastored the Sugar Land Baptist Church. *Baptist News Global* recounted excerpts from Lineberger's sermon four years earlier, delivered at the funeral of his friend, Pastor John Petty, pastor of Trinity Baptist Church in Kerrville, Texas, who also took his own life:

> Depression speaks a language of its own, known only to those who are depressed. Depression is both ancient and universal. In fact, those who study it—doctors and psychiatrists—tell us that depression is the most common emotional problem in America....No one is immune to it. It is not a willful fault, nor is it a sin....The Bible says we see through a glass darkly. We don't know how dark the darkness is in someone who is depressed. Through the darkened glass, they can't see the light of life or the love of others. They can only feel the pressure of the darkness of despair in their own mind. The darkness is visible to them and often invisible to us.[50]

In the same sermon, Pastor Lineberger discussed the fact that more Americans die by suicide than from war, cancer, and HIV/AIDS combined. It is a grim reality that four years after officiating the memorial of his friend who died by suicide, Pastor Lineberger ended his life. That decision affected not only his own life but also caused pain to his wife, Brenda, his three daughters, his ten grandchildren (with one more on the way), and the many people he served through the years in the pastorate.

"Another pastor commits suicide" is a headline, unfortunately, becoming more and more ubiquitous.[51] Pastor Robert McKeehan took his life a few days after the Sunday he preached on Romans 8:28: "*And we know that for those who love God all things work together for good, for those who are called according to his purpose.*" Described as an incredibly gifted teacher of God's Word, Robert had graduated from Dallas Theological Seminary with a Masters of Theology degree. He seemed to conceal his suicidal notions until that April day in 2014 when he hanged himself. The church he pastored reflected on his ministry by describing his passion to heal broken people through Jesus Christ, yet mourned the fact that he had been unable to find peace for his own brokenness. Tragically, there have been scores of deaths by suicide among pastors and their children throughout North America.

It is rare that people outside the immediate family discover all the personal facts of a person who completes suicide. Family members, generally, in sympathy, grief, and utter anguish, seldom disclose all the intricacies and challenges of the deceased person's life. Some suicides seem like a riddle and have no logical meaning. They leave us with the searing questions: *Why? Why didn't I see the signals? What was the trigger? What could I have done better?*

Far too often the average Christian feels ill-equipped to respond to a suicide. People who die by suicide leave friends and family members in a state of emotional and spiritual shock. Frequently, the reaction is to doubt God and ask, "Why did He allow this to happen?" That question almost has the implied tone "Why did God do this?" This is an understandable query but overlooks the fact that God created man with a free will. (The topics of evil, suffering, and pain will be addressed in the next lesson.) Furthermore, it omits an understanding of the facts involved in suicide.

Until you have been brought to the brink, you may not understand the intensity of another individual's struggle that might trigger a suicide attempt. God knows the internal struggle of our hearts. In a 2012 speech, Vice President Joe Biden reflected on the tragic death of his wife and young daughter: "For the first time in my life, I understood how someone could consciously decide to commit suicide...not because they were nuts. Because they'd been to the top of the mountain, and they just knew in their heart they'd never get there again."[52] The promise of Romans 8 tells us when we commit our lives to Christ, nothing can separate us from His love. The only sin that separates us from God is rejecting His Son as our Savior and Lord.

Individuals attempt suicide for a variety of reasons, and the people left behind often never fully understand why it happened. We do know, however, how much God values human life. He created us to have an abundant life; however, we have an enemy, who, *"like a roaring lion"* (1 Peter 5:8), has come into the world *"to steal and kill and destroy"* (John 10:10) our lives. Throughout the Bible, God provides us with principles for living a purposed life. While these principles may not prevent suicide in all cases, they are helpful and relevant for anyone dealing with a friend or loved one contemplating suicide or struggling with an invisible mental illness.

> *Above all else, guard your heart, for everything you do flows from it.*
> (Proverbs 4:23 NIV)

> *Do not conform to the pattern of this world, but be transformed by the renewing of your mind. Then you will be able to test and approve what God's will is—his good, pleasing and perfect will.*
> (Romans 12:2 NIV)

> *We demolish arguments and every pretension that sets itself up against the knowledge of God, and we take captive every thought to make it obedient to Christ.* (2 Corinthians 10:5 NIV)

Before you finish this chapter, several young people in North America will have attempted to take their own lives. Suicide is not acceptable and any one life lost is one too many. Most of the time, deaths by suicide will make news for a day and then be forgotten by the public. Family, friends, and acquaintances are left in the aftermath, facing years of fighting through a dense fog of uncertainty and anguish brought on by such a destructive act. They evaluate the circumstances and wonder, *Why did he die? Why did she take her own life?* Those doubts lead to speculation, and the speculation often leads to wrong conclusions. Misconceptions about suicide are prevalent.

The Suicide Epidemic

- Globally, one person dies every forty seconds by his or her own hand. (Further compelling data can be found at http://www.who.int/mental_health/suicide-prevention/en/.)

- Nearly one million people worldwide take their lives each year.
- Every fifteen minutes someone commits suicide in the US.
- Each year, twice as many US citizens kill themselves than kill one another.
- One in five completed suicides in the US involves a war veteran.
- Males take their lives at nearly five times the rate of females and represent more than 80 percent of all US suicides.
- Suicide rates for females are highest among women aged 45–54.
- Suicide is the second leading cause of death among college students.
- Suicide is the third leading cause of death among people aged 15–24.
- Suicide is the fourth leading cause of death among people aged 10–14.
- For every person who takes their own life, there are twenty-five unsuccessful suicide attempts.

For more information and statistics on suicide visit these helpful websites:
http://www.cdc.gov/ViolencePrevention/pdf/Suicide_DataSheet-a.pdf
https://www.dosomething.org/facts/11-facts-about-suicide
http://www.save.org/index.cfm?fuseaction=home.viewPage&page_id=705D5DF4-055B-F1EC-3F66462866FCB4E6

Can a Christian Complete Suicide?

The obvious answer is yes. An authentic Christian in disobedience can steal, murder, lie, and grieve the Lord in any number of ways. The distinction, however, of a genuine Christian is that they cannot habitually sin without experiencing spiritual discipline and correction from the Lord. (See Hebrews 12:5–11.) The seventh commandment is "*You shall not murder*" (Exodus 20:13). The Bible teaches that life is a gift from God, and only He has the authority to end a human life. A Christian can commit any sin known to man. A Christian can be chronically depressed. As we will see throughout part 3 of this book, many Christians suffer from a myriad of mental illnesses. If you do, you are not alone. Just because a person has received Jesus Christ as their Savior does not eradicate their choice in behaviors, their hereditary traits, nor their biological, mental, and emotional states.

It is hard to forget many of our first experiences: riding a bike, a first kiss, taking Dad's car out for a spin, our wedding day, the birth of a child, or our salvation experience. When one goes into pastoral ministry, invariably you will have your first experience of not only preaching, but also marrying and burying congregants. I have had my share of blunders in ministry. For example, I once pronounced the husband and wife by the bride's name rather than that of the groom. It is hard to dismiss these memories from one's mind! The first funeral I officiated was a suicide. I will never forget my first personal experience dealing with the fallout of suicide on the family that has been left behind.

At forty-three, Kim was in the prime of her life and a devout Christian who regularly attended our church. She was married with four beautiful children, a lover of animals, and nominated by the local school district as Teacher of the Year, having taught for twenty years. Kim struggled with chronic depression and one day, she saw no way out, went into the woods, and committed suicide. In the aftermath I was with the family trying to pick up the pieces. The "Why" questions never end. Her funeral service was packed with hundreds of mournful friends honoring her life, yet the hope of Jesus was presented. My experience with Kim and her family awakened me to the stark reality of mental illness—the invisible illness—within our church families, a reality we rarely hear addressed from the pulpit.

As I stated above, worldwide, nearly one million people complete suicide each year. Every fifteen minutes someone commits suicide in the United States. Globally, one person dies every forty seconds by his or her own hand.[53] More US citizens kill themselves than kill one another each year, stark evidence that we are all far more dangerous to ourselves than we are to other people. In fact, there are twice as many suicides as murders. One in five suicides in the US is a war veteran. In the US, twenty-two veterans, more than eight thousand vets per year, complete suicide each day.[54] Males take their own lives at nearly five times the rate of females and represent more than 80 percent of all US suicides. Middle-aged men, 45–64 years of age, are at highest risk.[55] Suicide has reached epidemic levels. Yet suicide is preventable. Unfortunately, most people do not know where to start.

Do Christians Who Die By Suicide Go to Hell?

Suicide is wrong. Suicide forever harms not only the victim but also his or her immediate circle of family and friends. It is a selfish act. Notwithstanding, there is no passage anywhere in the Bible that supports the view that a follower of Jesus who commits suicide goes to hell. Some people incorrectly believe that suicide is the "unforgiveable sin," but this is not a biblical teaching. Remember, God forgives *all* sin, except that of rejecting Jesus Christ as Lord and Savior. The salvation we receive from Jesus Christ is eternal, regardless of our mental state or our spiritual maturity or immaturity. The apostle Paul wrote, *"In Him you also trusted, after you heard the word of truth, the gospel of your salvation; in whom also, having believed, you were* ***sealed*** *with the Holy Spirit of promise"* (Ephesians 1:13 NKJV). The "seal" in biblical times referred to a finished transaction, complete ownership. When we received Christ as Savior we were, in a sense, "locked in" to God's family by the substitutionary death that Jesus Christ endured for us on the cross. In addition, we are indwelt with the Holy Spirit at the moment of our salvation and have the spiritual capacity to live a life above the power of sin. Romans 6:14: *"For sin shall not have dominion over you, for you are not under law but under grace* (NKJV)."

There is no question, for a believer to die by suicide is a poor testimony, regardless of the situation. God is the author of life, and only He can bring a life to its conclusion. God said,

> *Today I have given you the choice between life and death, between blessings and curses. Now I call on heaven and earth to witness the choice you make. Oh, that you would choose life, so that you and your descendants might live! You can make this choice by loving the Lord your God, obeying him, and committing yourself firmly to him. This is the key to your life.* (Deuteronomy 30:19–20 NLT)

God desires us to follow Him and He will bless us with purpose and lasting fulfillment. God heals the brokenhearted and binds up their wounds. (See Psalm 147:3.) "*We are afflicted in every way, but not crushed; perplexed, but not to despair; persecuted, but not forsaken; struck down, but not destroyed*" (2 Corinthians 4:8–9). Our Savior cries out to us, saying, "*Come to me, all you who are weary and burdened, and I will give you rest*" (Matthew 11:28 NIV). Yes, suicide does happen, increasingly so, even among pastors and other Christians. We will never completely understand and we may not always be able to answer the "Why" question satisfactorily, but we must understand that it does happen and learn how to respond with compassion and grace.

God's people have always been a people of waiting. In Old Testament times, faithful Jews waited for the Messiah to come to earth; today, we await His Second Coming, when He will make all things new. (See Revelation 21:5.) In that time we, as believers, will be with God in a place where "*there will be no more death or mourning or crying or pain, for the old order of things has passed away*" (verses 4–5 NIV). Until then, as we wait, we "*groan inwardly*" (Romans 8:23) in the present sufferings of a world and church that is marred by sin. We are weak of body and mind, but we have a faithful promise and gift: "*the Spirit helps us in our weakness*" (verse 26).

Pastor and blogger Stephen Altrogge wrote,

> Until the day Jesus returns, I will live in a body which does not function as God originally intended. My brain, which is a key, central, integral part of my body, will not function correctly. Chemicals will become imbalanced. Serotonin will not be properly absorbed. Norepinephrine will be unevenly distributed. Synapses won't fire correctly. My brain, just like every other part of my body, is prone to illness.[56]

How to Intervene

I learned about suicide and its far-reaching collateral damage when I was very young. Since the early 1980s, my father, Dr. Jerry Johnston, after decades of speaking to hundreds of thousands of students and interacting personally with so many of them, has been widely considered to be an expert on the suicide epidemic in North America. He wrote a popular book *Why Suicide?* (Thomas Nelson, 1987) and has worked closely with suicidology experts and mental health professionals, who have also provided a unique perspective on intervention and coping with loss. With his permission I will share some of the concepts he has learned and shared with me that have been equally effective for suicidal people in my own ministry.

Growing up it was a regular occurrence to receive letters from people who had heard my father speak on the issue of suicide and then chose life instead of their own self-inflicted death. Dad's perspective was also unique in that he himself had attempted suicide as a teenager. As a survivor of suicide, he was always motivated to help others. Therefore, our family was also committed to minister to other families impacted by suicide. For the last fifteen years in both ministry and higher education, I have made use of all of these combined factors to dissuade congregants and students from suicide. This section is dedicated to saving lives and ministering to those who have suffered loss. At several key points I will lean on what I have learned, observed, and participated in with the hope that these principles will give you the courage to intervene when necessary.

Every time a person dies by their own hand there is, as suicidologists teach, a contagion effect. When someone dies by suicide it not uncommon for a spouse, a father, mother, brother, sister, or friend to make a similar attempt at taking their own life. Sensationalizing suicide in the media is also problematic and can cause troubled individuals to mimic such an attempt. We refer to these chain-reaction suicides as "copycat suicides." This phenomenon has also been codified as "the cluster effect." We have seen this illustrated in many high schools across the nation, where teens attempt suicide after a classmate has successfully done so. Before the National Institute of Mental Health briefed national and local media and other professionals on this danger, it was common for newspaper articles and television reports to go into great detail when covering suicides, profiling the victim and showing their picture. Far too often, copycat attempts followed. Armed with the information of "the cluster effect," the media has become more circumspect in their reporting and copycat attempts have dropped sharply. The rare exception is when well-known celebrities take their own lives, such as comedian Robin Williams, who, battling depression and lamenting the onset of Parkinson's disease, hung himself in a bedroom closet.[57]

Talking intelligently about suicide will not cause it to occur, but it can prevent it from happening. Failing to talk about suicide may have disastrous consequences. You may not be an expert, but your care and compassion are essential. Know the facts and not the fallacies about suicide.

Read and respond to each statement below.

True or False: Talking about suicide will plant the idea in a depressed person's mind.

True or False: People who talk about suicide usually do not follow through with it.

True or False: Most suicides occur without warning.

True or False: When depression lifts, suicide is no longer a concern.

True or False: A suicidal person cannot be talked out of it if he or she is intent on dying.

True or False: Only certain people are the suicidal type.

True or False: African American men complete suicide at the same rates as Caucasian men.

True or False: Only insane or "crazy" people complete suicide.

True or False: Women threaten suicide but only men complete suicide.

True or False: If a person has survived a suicide attempt, the likelihood of a second attempt is diminished.

True or False: People who complete suicide have not sought medical help prior to the attempt.

True or False: Suicide is a new phenomenon. No one in the Bible attempted or completed suicide.

All of these statements are false, and yet many of them are common fallacies.[58]

There are five specific action steps to implement when you notice someone close to you is talking about suicide or exhibiting signs of suicidal ideation. Here is a strategy of compassion, concern, and intervention:

Step One: ***Listen and observe the person carefully.***

This relates to the engagement principle "Shut Up and Listen" we will see later, in chapter 10. Please do not dominate the conversation or preach at the wounded person. Emotions are raw when a person is suicidal. Think of how gently you would respond to someone if they had a broken arm, wrist, or leg. Approach the person emotionally with the same care, calmness, and attentiveness. Ask the suicidal person to explain to you what is bothering them. Let them talk. Even though it is difficult, remain calm; listen and look the person in the eyes. Frequently when someone is suicidal they are also self-medicating with drugs and/or alcohol. When a friend or family member is drug dependent they are communicating to you with their behavior and not only their words. No one desires to be an enabler who encourages self-destructive behavior in other people, but in their ignorance, many people do just that. When you witness people self-medicating, say something. Care enough not to allow the addiction to get worse and worse, year after year. A suicidal individual is counting on us to go the extra mile by carefully observing them, listening to their words, and loving them enough to intervene. Listen, listen, listen, and then keep listening.

Step Two: ***Identify with the hurting person.***

If you do not identify with the suicidal person (son, daughter, wife, husband, or friend) there is a much higher risk you will lose them to suicide.

Do not add to their sense of guilt by suggesting that if they were closer with God they would not be having suicidal thoughts. That is a myth. A Christian who is too busy being a judgmental Pharisee overlooks the fact that statistically most people have entertained a momentary or perhaps more prolonged thought of suicide in times of intense stress.

Step Three: ***Initiate a loving, calculated response (being very careful and sensitive).***

Ignoring the suicidal person is the worst possible scenario. Perhaps you were raised in a family that never addressed the issue and always swept unpleasantries under the rug. That is *dysfunction*. A healthy person will be the architect of healing for a friend or family member who is struggling with suicidal thoughts. Saving your family member or friends will involve you interrupting your normal schedule. That is okay. Remember, most people spell love T-I-M-E. Invest time in creating an action plan to bring the person out of the depths of their suicidal struggle.

Step Four: ***Ask the key question.***

Whenever you suspect that someone close to you is contemplating taking his or her life, an essential question must be asked: ***Do you have a plan or method to take your life? Have you considered an actual time to do it?*** If they have a plan, method, or timeline, they are in immediate danger. Stay with the hurting individual at all times. They should never be left alone. You must also commit to the time and expense of professional help. You do not need to lead the person to healing alone. Perhaps the person might need to be hospitalized. I always encourage a reputable, Christian-based counselor and/or psychiatrist or a trained, experienced pastor to lead an intervention with specific healing steps.

Step Five: ***Access the National Suicide Prevention Lifeline.***

Prevention, prevention, prevention. The phone number for the National Suicide Prevention Lifeline is 1-800-273-TALK (8255). Be certain to "like" the National Suicide Prevention Lifeline Facebook page: www.facebook.com/800273TALK. This phenomenal organization interfaces with Facebook to geographically pinpoint suicidal notions using online comments in order to provide assistance. It is an excellent resource and I heartily commend it to you.

No one is unaffected by mental illness. If you have not personally struggled with mental illness or thoughts of suicide, chances are your friend, spouse, children, coworker, or neighbor have. As Christians, we need to build awareness of the problem and remove the stigma, because mental illness is widespread and affects everyone. The ministry of Jesus focused on removing barriers to belief and restoring people who were suffering.

During a sermon series in 2013, "Surviving Tough Times," by Pastor Rick Warren, his son Matthew completed suicide. After a pleasant dinner with his parents, he returned to his home in Mission Viejo, California, and died of a self-inflicted gunshot. After this tragedy Pastor Warren sent an Email to the Saddleback Church staff:

> No words can express the anguished grief we feel right now. Our youngest son, Matthew, age 27, and a lifelong member of Saddleback, died today. You who watched Matthew grow up knew he was an incredibly kind, gentle, and compassionate man. He had a brilliant intellect and a gift for sensing who was most in pain or most uncomfortable in a room. He'd then make a beeline to that person to engage and encourage them. But only those closest knew that he struggled from birth with mental illness, dark holes of depression, and even suicidal thoughts. In spite of America's best doctors, meds, counselors, and prayers for healing, the torture of mental illness never subsided. Today, after a fun evening together with Kay and me, in a momentary wave of despair at his home, he took his life. Kay and I often marveled at his courage to keep moving in spite of relentless pain. I'll never forget how, many years ago, after another approach had failed to give relief, Matthew said, "Dad, I know I'm going to heaven. Why can't I just die and end this pain?" but he kept going for another decade.[59]

We can no longer save Matthew Warren, but we can save others. In truth, this very minute, there is a sincere Christian—a Matthew Warren—who is struggling with suicide or an associated mental illnesses. To answer the broader unanswered questions of mental illness sweeping our churches we now turn.

9

"PLEASE LEAVE OUR CHURCH" AND OTHER DISASTERS: REMOVING THE STIGMA THAT THE MENTALLY ILL ARE NOT WELCOME AT CHURCH

ne of the most popular movies of 2015 was *American Sniper,* based on the life of Chris Kyle, a Navy SEAL

sniper who set records for number of kills while in combat. After four tours in Iraq, this married father of two clearly experienced psychological fallout from battle stress, or PTSD (post-traumatic stress disorder). As he attempted to reinsert himself into civilian life, he suffered from nightmares of battlefield flashbacks. A patient wife and wise physician directed Chris to help other marines by listening to their wartime stories and, in many cases, observing the physical and emotional handicaps they inherited from severe, nightmarish combat missions and the death of comrades in battle. It was while undergoing this recovery that Chris and close friend Chad Littlefield were shot to death at a gun range by Eddie Ray Routh, a former marine who was mentally ill. Following the box-office success of *American Sniper*, a nationwide conversation about mental illness ensued, a conversation we need to have in the church, as well. *Forbes* magazine reported that mental illness costs employers between $79–105 billion annually in indirect costs: "The way employees think, feel, and behave can impact everything from productivity and communication to their ability to maintain safety."[60] What cannot be measured is the harmful effect of the church's collective silence toward, and avoidance of, the mentally ill. The sad reality is that when a church member is brave enough to admit a personal struggle with mental illness, they often risk being ostracized from their faith community. The Christian church has become a community of denial, suffering from this invisible disease in silence.

The Church of Invisible Diseases

She calls it her "invisible handicap." Why? Because while mental illness is very real, constantly holding her back, weighing her down, and obliterating her self-esteem, those around her fail to see or recognize this disease that is so real to her. My friend Anna is twenty-two years old and one of the most courageous people I know. She has spent half her life struggling with mental illness, and now she is speaking out about it. Anna's story is mirrored by so many people in our churches who are struggling silently, dying on the inside. Anna does not fit the typical stereotype of what struggling with a mental illness is supposed to look like. Anna comes from a wonderful Christian home; her parents and four siblings are committed followers of Jesus, active in their local church and serving their community. She is talented, educated, articulate, and from the outside, you would never guess she struggles with anything.

It all began for Anna when she was diagnosed with type 1 juvenile diabetes. Her health spiraled into years of anxiety, depression, and ultimately, a debilitating eating disorder. It might surprise you to learn that research shows that eating disorders are the most fatal of all mental illnesses.

Anna was kind enough to share her story with me:

> Anna: I never realized I was depressed, I never even thought of depression, probably because no one ever talked about it!

Anna's mental illness caused her to feel like she had no control over her body. She would force herself to look at herself in the mirror, which caused her to cry and become angry with God. *How could God curse me with this dysfunctional, disgusting body?* Anna thought. Going to church only made things worse. When the congregation stood to sing, she was so embarrassed by her body that she wasn't able to worship. She did not want anyone to see her. Anna even refused to take communion, obsessed with counting every single calorie. Her mental illness made her feel like such a failure as a Christian.

> Anna: No one ever talked to me about my mental illness, none of my teachers, no sermons from my pastors, or my youth group leaders; and my parents never talked with me about it.

Anna's eating disorder (and all the associated depression and anxiety) consumed her thoughts and as she says, "They took everything from me."

> Anna: I lost connection with all of my friends; I pushed everyone away, broke up with my boyfriend, lost faith in God, and I was taken away from a job I loved. I had prayed to God for help, but felt like He hadn't heard me. I never got better, no matter how hard I prayed. I was sick of praying about it.

An intervention by Anna's parents and psychiatrist saved her life. Her participation in an inpatient treatment center began her road to recovery as she began the healing process from the inside out.

> Anna: Once my brain was properly nourished, I realized that it was not my fault; my anxiety, depression, mental illness and eating disorder did not make me a bad person, or a failure as a Christian. I had a medical condition and needed professional help! I can't help but wonder, if I had learned about depression, anxiety, and mental disorders growing up, maybe I would have seen red flags sooner and asked for help. But how could I seek help for a problem I didn't know I had?

Stop the Silence

When you read the words *mental illness* what pictures or words immediately come into your mind? Most people stigmatize the mentally ill as people in hospital gowns indefinitely committed to a psych ward. But that is an inaccurate depiction of someone with a mental illness. Would it surprise you to learn that people with mental illnesses worship at your church and attend Bible study class with you? Knowing that, it's particularly unfortunate that we say so little about mental illness in the church. We act as if it does not exist. It leaves Christian leaders in a quandary, because we know that almost every family has a least one person suffering from some type of mental illness.

A Stark Reality

The National Institute of Mental Health reports mental illnesses are common in our country as evidenced by the following data:

- Depression is the leading cause of disability world.[61]
- In 2012, there were an estimated 9.6 million adults, 18 or older, in the US with Serious Mental Illness (SMI) in the past year.

- In 2012, there were an estimated 43.7 million adults, 18 and older, in the US with a mental illness in the past year. (This is significant: one in five adult Americans suffer from a mental illness.)
- More than 20 percent of children, either currently or at some point during their lives, have had a serious, debilitating mental disorder.
- Major depression is one of the most common disorders in the US.
- One in twenty Americans live with serious mental illness: bipolar, schizophrenia, PTSD, or chronic depression.
- In 2012, an estimated 16 million adults, 18 or older, in the US had at least one major depressive episode in the past year.
- In 2012, an estimated 2.2 million adolescents, ages 12–17, in the US had at least one major depressive episode in the past year.
- Forty-eight percent, or nearly half the world's population, will have a direct experience with mental illness themselves over the course of their lifetime.[62]

The number one problem in our churches related to matters of mental health and mental disorders is silence. Statistics prove that one in four people suffer from mental illness. Invisible illnesses of the brain have the power to isolate you, cause you to cease to be a productive member of society, and shorten your lifespan. Mental illness is not a choice, but the good news is that it is treatable. No one is unaffected by mental illness. As Christians, we need to build awareness of the problem and remove the stigma, because mental illness is widespread and affects everyone. The National Alliance of Mental Illness says that only 20–40 percent of people struggling with mental illnesses are productively employed, mostly due to shame and stigma.[63] The church has this elephant in the room called mental illness. It fills our churches each Sunday, yet no one feels comfortable talking about it. The ministry of Jesus focused on removing barriers to belief and restoring people who were suffering: "*When Jesus heard this, he told them, 'Healthy people don't need a doctor—sick people do. I have come to call not those who think they are righteous, but those who know they are sinners'*" (Mark 2:17 NLT).

Dr. Ed Stetzer, executive director of LifeWay Research, recently remarked at a conference with the Leadership Network on "Mental Health and the Church": "We need to stop whispering in our churches about mental illness!" Amen! LifeWay Research produced survey results in their report "Serving Those with Mental Illness," which stated that 66 percent of pastors rarely or never address the subject of mental illness from their pulpits. The same survey revealed the majority of churchgoers wish their pastors would address mental illness more often. Even more striking, 23 percent of pastors say they have personally struggled with mental illness.

The Bible has much to say about mental health, right thinking, and loving God with our mind. In response to the expert in the law who asked Jesus which of the commandments was the greatest, Jesus replied, *"You shall love the Lord your God with all your heart and with all your soul and with all your mind"* (Matthew 22:37, see also 2 Timothy 1:7; Isaiah 26:3; 1 Peter 5:7; Romans 12:2). What is lost in that passage is the commandment to love God with our minds, our intellect, our thinking. The Bible discusses mental health; so should the church, *regularly*.

Stop the Shame and Exclusion

Prior to entering higher education I had the privilege to pastor a church for over a decade. I will never forget the time I was meeting with a new family who informed me that they had joined our church after their previous church had asked them to leave because of a family member with mental illness. Too often, instead of integrating and assimilating those who struggling with a mental illness, we segregate and exclude them. We may not mean to, but in this process we shame people who don't deserve it.

My expertise in scholarship is the Gospels and the life of Jesus, and I can assure you that as a Bible scholar, I never see Jesus banishing a hurting person in His ministry. Mental illness is isolating. Those who suffer feel cut off from the church and abandoned by God. People with sick brains may not simply be "fixed" at the altar by a passionate prayer or anointing oil. Does God heal? Absolutely. Does He work miracles? Absolutely. But just as we have people who continue to struggle with physical problems, there are also those people who continue to struggle with mental/emotional problems. We must avoid shaming them. God has not given us a spirit of fear or of cowardice; He has given us the Holy Spirit, who gives us God's power to train ourselves to think rightly, to love and to have self-control. (See 2 Timothy 1:7.) Jesus' ministry and the manifestation of the kingdom of God was focused on healing broken people. That is the task Jesus gave the church—heal broken people. Did you know that individuals experiencing psychological distress are more likely to seek help from a pastor before any other professional? We need to be prepared.

Understand Mental Illness and Be Present

As a church community we need to understand mental illness and be present. Peter Jennings, the former ABC news anchor, was known for always showing up. In fact, he said the secret to life is "showing up." The church needs to "show up," as it relates to mental illness. One of the most attractive aspects of the church is the element of community. The reality of the church is that we believe together, we grow together, we hurt together, and we suffer together. Mental illness happens not just to that person or family who is struggling, it happens to the entire body of Christ. Jesus did not say "on this strong Christian, who reads his Bible every day, I will build My church, and the gates of hell will not prevail against it." No, in Matthew 16:18, in response to Peter's declaration of a Jesus-centric faith, He said *"on this **rock**"*—this truth—*"I will build my church, and the gates of hell shall not prevail against it."* The church is the ark of safety.

We begin to understand mental illness by properly defining it. Most people do not really know what it is. Mental illness is defined as a physical dysfunction of the brain that causes the inability to think or feel or act in a person's normal manner. Outside of a miracle, an individual does not get out of bed in the morning and speak away high cholesterol; similarly, one cannot pray away mental illness. There are treatment procedures for physical problems of the body (i.e. cholesterol levels) and there are treatments for the unseen illnesses of the brain. Mental and physical health should be treated as equal.

The Church Is an Essential Player in Treating Mental Illness

Babe Ruth once said, "It's hard to beat a person who never gives up." The church should never give up on, cast aside, or push out the mentally ill. The church needs to take her responsibility to the frontlines, ministering to all those who've been afflicted. For far too long the "bride of Christ" been absent from the equation in serving the mentally ill. I pray that you will become more sensitive to those people in your life who are in the midst of this struggle.

I enjoy watching TED Talks while I exercise. In her talk "What's So Funny about Mental Illness?" Ruby Wax made the point that all diseases, except those of the brain, garner sympathy from people.[64] Why is it that diseases and injuries of every part of your body illicit compassion from friends and loved ones, but not so much for sickness of the brain? While not agreeing with some of her conclusions, I transposed some of her thoughts and projected them on the church. Think about it. Our church families are so helpful when someone is sick or a family member suffers from a long-term illness. Schedules are created so that a hurting person is never left alone. Meals are delivered. Pastors make visits. Why does the church not spring into action when someone is suffering from a mental illness?

There are some exceptionally helpful support groups and organizations dedicated to helping people with mental illness, but most of them are not Christian-based. Why is it that the church has fallen behind in providing support and treatment for the mentally ill? Dr. Daniel Moorehead is a Christian psychiatrist examining the clinical side of the brain, and he said, "Mental illness is nobody's fault....Mental illness is not a matter of choice or of willpower. It is a matter of can't rather than won't."[65] I would add that mental illness is not a spiritual problem, either. You do not develop a mental illness because you lack faith. Believing more will not cure mental illness.

I return to the conversation with my courageous friend Anna.

Anna: Through therapy and recovery I have learned that mental illness does not make me a failure as a person or a failure as a Christian. Recovery from my eating disorder, anxiety, and depression is a long-term battle. There is no silver bullet. Many days I do not feel like fighting my disordered thoughts, it is exhausting! But, I know God loves me enough to send His Son to die for me. Remembering this helps me want to love myself! If I can't do it for me, I can do it for Him.

Anna finished our interview with the most powerful concluding thought:

Anna: Opening up and sharing about my mental illnesses has been such a huge part of my recovery. Hiding my depression, anxiety, and eating disorder gave these illnesses so much power over me. I am no longer a slave to my eating disorder, and with God's strength, I can walk upright and free!

The Healing Equation

Admit that every family struggles. We're all broken. We're all messed up. We need to reach out to one another and begin an honest conversation. We need to change our thinking as the church. How can we deal with this together rather than looking at people struggling with a mental disorder as a problem?

Love instead of judge, condemn, and misunderstand. One of the funny observations I made very early in my ministry is that Christians don't gossip—they share prayer requests. That is a joke but it is funny because there is truth in it. One of the reasons we do not discuss mental problems in the church is due to a fear of people gossiping and ostracizing us. We have lost our first love. John 13:35: *"By this all people will know that you are my disciples, if you have love for one another."*

Build support groups for every age level in our church that address mental disorders. Mental illness does not separate people from the love of God, and it shouldn't separate us from the love of our church, either. If you look at the studies, one of the boldest myths is that children are not affected by mental illness. Did you know mental illness among every age category is increasing? We need to educate ourselves. Some of the most successful Christians I know regularly engage in Christian counseling or therapy.

I learned from my conversation with Anna that one of the most helpful things in her recovery was being surrounding by positive, supportive people who discussed mental illness instead of ignoring its existence. Experiencing community is a major part of the treatment process. We can encourage those with mental disorders to have appropriate boundaries and practice coping mechanisms. We can help identify professionals within the mental health arena who base their treatment on a biblical worldview.

Encourage the mentally ill to serve within our church communities! Most people struggling with a mental illness are extremely witty, good-humored, and highly intelligent. It is an often-overlooked fact that some of the greatest Christians of all time have had lifelong struggles with depression, thoughts of suicide, and mental illness.

When my wife and I lived in Oxford, England, at the encouragement of my friend, Mike, we traveled about an hour away to a little town known as Olney, a place that may sound familiar because it is there that John Newton, preparing for a Bible study on New Year's Day 1773, wrote perhaps the most famous hymn of all time: "Amazing Grace." It was published a few years later in the now-famous book *The Olney Hymns,* but many are not aware that the hymnbook had a coauthor, John Newton's dear friend, William Cowper, who himself wrote nearly seventy of the three hundred or so hymns. You've no doubt sung the hymns like "There Is a Fountain, Filled with Blood" or "O for a Closer Walk with God." Aside from being John Newton's best friend, William Cowper is remembered as one of the great poets of the eighteenth century. Benjamin Franklin cherished Cowper's poems. A window at the great Westminster Abbey honors him.

Cowper struggled with paralyzing depression his entire life. He attempted suicide numerous times. His depression was chronic, and before meeting John Newton, Cowper spent years at St. Albans Insane Asylum before relocating to Olney. The local pastor in Olney was John Newton, thus the two men became friends. Even though he was afflicted with so much mental illness, he wrote beautifully comforting lines.

You've most likely used a line from Cowper's hymns with John Newton, without even knowing it:

God moves in a mysterious way
His wonders to perform;
He plants His footsteps in the sea
And rides upon the storm.[66]

Mental illness touches us all. We can learn from the examples of John Newton, who rescued his friend by simply being there, supporting him, loving him in his mental illness, and, ultimately, by putting him to work writing hymns. As we close this chapter, where do you find yourself in the story? Perhaps you are a John Newton and you have a friend or family member you need to walk with. Our church is filled with William Cowpers, talented people, struggling with mental illness. Let's commit to God that invisible diseases will be invisible no longer. Rather than asking a family struggling with mental illness to leave our church, let us integrate them into our communities of faith.

10

ENGAGEMENT PRINCIPLE #2: SHUT UP AND LISTEN

Flying on Delta Airlines was part of my childhood. Traveling with my dad from church to church in his evangelistic ministry gave me the opportunity to achieve Medallion status as a fourteen-year-old, with fifty-six segments in a single year. The most valuable possession in my wallet was my Delta Medallion membership card! Needless to say, I have flown in airplanes of all shapes and sizes. It never ceases to amaze me how the vast majority of airline passengers never listen to the preflight safety demonstration. If you've flown, you know that this is the presentation in which the flight attendants demonstrate how to operate a seatbelt (nothing earth shattering here), explain that passengers must comply with lighted signs and smoking bans, warn about the possible dropping of oxygen masks, and point out the locations of the exit doors.

When it comes to sharing our faith, some Christians resemble the aloof airline passengers completely ignoring the most important message, should the plane experience an emergency requiring an emergency exit, not to mention survival. In his *Harvard Business Review* article "If You Want People to Listen, Stop Talking," Peter Bregman points out that words are sneaky, in that they can easily get in the way of a conversation.[67] The principle of closing our mouths and listening to a different perspective gives us the right to eventually be heard. A faith dialogue should always begin with the other person's perspective, spiritually speaking, not our own. Since we live in a post-/anti-Christian culture, I do not begin a conversation about Christianity with the Bible or by quoting Scripture. (See Part 5: Bible-*ish* Christianity: Why Most Christians Know Just Enough about the Bible to Be Dangerous.)

Many people struggle at being good listeners. Perhaps you have found yourself in a conversation in which, while you are talking, you realize that the other person is not really listening but instead preparing for what they are going to say next. It is remarkable what people will say to you when they know you are sincerely listening. We learn by listening. Perception is reality when answering the unanswered questions of Christianity. Offering your opinion first (even if well-informed) is a subtle form of intellectual terrorism, in that it shows an utter disregard for what the person might be thinking or feeling toward God or Christianity. Proverbs 10:19 states, "*When words are many, transgression is not lacking, but whoever restrains his lips is prudent.*" This verse is a wise reminder that talking too much in a conversation can lead to sin! James certainly encouraged less talking and more listening, "*The tongue also is a fire, a world of evil among the parts of the body. It corrupts the whole body, sets the whole course of one's life on fire, and is itself set on fire by hell*" (James 3:6 NIV). If a tongue "*is a fire,*" some Christians resemble fire-breathing dragons. James begins his epistle with an exhortation: "*Know this, my beloved brothers: let every person be quick to hear, slow to speak, slow to anger*" (James 1:19). The conscientious Christian is careful and quick to listen.

Furthermore, your posture should be open and inviting. You are inquisitive to hear what this person has to say, you ask follow-up questions, and you give both verbal and nonverbal clues that you hear what they're saying, even if you disagree. You put the other person above yourself and your need to win an argument at all costs.

How would you rate your listening skills? When you are conversing with a friend about God do you know their pressure points? A lot of people crash and burn in witnessing because they have not bothered to observe the landlines of the conversation. Do you know what barriers are holding them back? Do you interrupt? Body language should also be monitored when we listen compassionately. Resist folding your arms. Be aware of your facial expression. For the love of God, use a breath mint!

Listening, which includes not talking, is the key ingredient in an effective witness for Jesus Christ. Listening requires time, and we usually don't have much time in our day and age. Listening should be perfected as an essential technique as you share the gospel of Jesus Christ. When you listen to the other person they feel that you actually care enough about them so that they can be heard. Eventually that person will say something like "Jeremiah, I have been dominating the conversation! I'm the one doing all of the talking. I want to hear what you think."

Yes, we have a story to tell when we share evidences or answer unanswered questions about the Christian faith. However, our launching point in the conversation should be at the intersection of the other person's point of need, not in retreading the tires of tired, one-size-fits-all witnessing.

PART 4

PARANORMALCY: UNDERSTANDING THE PARANORMAL ALLURE AMONG CHRISTIANS AND HOW TO ESCAPE IT

11

VAMPIRES, ZOMBIES, GHOSTS, MEDIUMS, AND PARANORMAL PHENOMENON HAVE NEVER BEEN MORE NORMAL OR PROFITABLE

Oren Peli was an up and coming software programmer living in San Diego, California. Originally from Israel, Peli came to the United States at the age of nineteen. No stranger to hard work and innovation, he quickly grabbed his slice of the American Dream and moved into his first home, but he was not used to living so far away from family or friends in a neighborhood that was so eerily quiet. Oren said he was uncomfortable because he heard strange noises at night—creaks and knocks all over the house that would startle and scare him. The thirty-seven-year-old programmer had no experience with movies or the film industry, but he didn't live far from Hollywood and had an idea. Oren put an ad on a website, hired some unknown actors for five hundred dollars each, and invested fifteen thousand dollars of his own money to produce a movie with his home video camera. He later joked that if the movie was a bomb, at least he had added some new hardwood flooring to his home for the occasion. Oren wrote a screenplay about a young couple, Katie and Micah, who moved into a home that, like Oren's, also made strange noises, but this home was haunted by a demon. As the plot unfolds, Katie and Micah decide to set up a movie camera to record and document the activity that occurred in their home as they slept. That "activity" became the box-office sensation *Paranormal Activity*.

At first DreamWorks executives were hesitant to purchase a film made with unknown actors, shot Handycam style by an equally unknown writer/director by night and software programmer by day. Steven Spielberg was undecided, but after watching the micro-budget DVD of *Paranormal Activity* at his Pacific Palisades estate, strange phenomena occurred inside his home. Spielberg had to hire a locksmith after a door to an empty bedroom mysteriously became locked from the inside.[68] Spielberg returned the DVD to the studio sealed in a garbage bag, intent on DreamWorks releasing the film. It was scary, original, and hit home.

Initially DreamWorks executives were alarmed because moviegoers were walking out of the preview screenings. Then they discovered that people were not leaving out of boredom, but because they were so scared they could not finish the movie.[69] The rest of the story is something of Hollywood lore. The little film that was shot in just seven days was theatrically released two years later, in 2009. *Entertainment Weekly*'s article, "'Paranormal Activity': A marketing campaign so ingenious it's scary," highlighted the success of the grassroots marketing appeal, in which fans could vote online to bring the movie to their community.[70] The mass appeal was encouraged by the fact that trailers for *Paranormal Activity* did not show the actual movie, only the frightful reactions of audiences watching it. The trailer went viral online. Fans of the film spoke proudly of not being able to sleep for a week after seeing it.

The original film grossed nearly $200 million worldwide, making *Paranormal Activity* the most profitable movie of all time, with a mind boggling 1.2 million percent return on investment.[71] This proves that paranormal activity—a genre that was once called the occult and thought to be strangely alluring only the fringes of society—has gone mainstream.

I think paranormal activity became more culturally attractive largely because of a movie that was released as I was graduating high school. All of my friends saw it numerous times. I saw it. No movie captured the intrigue of youth and catapulted millennials into paranormal interest more than M. Night Shyamalan's *The Sixth Sense*, with its iconic line: "I see dead people." What followed was an entertainment industry lured by dollars and possessed by the notion of vampires, zombies, ghost hunters, UFO conspiracies, and a host of other ghostly adaptations created for both the small and big screens.

The Paranormal Is Attractive and Has Become Normative in Society

The Lincoln Bedroom within the White House is a bit of a misnomer, because the sixteenth president of the United States never actually slept there. Rather, it served as his study and office.[72] During a World War II visit to the White House, Winston Churchill walked into the Lincoln Bedroom following a lengthy bath. Wearing nothing but a cigar, Churchill claimed that when he entered the room he saw the ghost of Abraham Lincoln leaning against the fireplace.[73] The story goes that Churchill said to the ghost, "Good evening, Mr. President. You seem to have me at a disadvantage."[74] Ghost stories are similar to urban legends in that almost everyone has a tale or version to share, which has contributed to their mass appeal.

The paranormal has emerged as a massive industry: television series, movie franchises, best-selling novels, haunted houses, ghost hunters, poltergeist tours, fortune-telling, channeling, psychic fairs, ghost photography, UFO sightings and alleged abductions, government conspiracies, Big Foot, and even the Loch Ness Monster. To cogently answer the unanswered questions related to paranormal phenomena, we must first understand its appeal, even among Christians. Our aim should be to emulate the leaders from Issachar, *"And of Issachar, men who had understanding of the times to know what Israel ought to do, 200 chiefs; and all their kinsmen were under their command"* (1 Chronicles 12:32 NKJV). Hollywood's entertainment investors are betting on your attraction to the paranormal, and their bets historically have paid off. Significant dollars are being made capitalizing on the trendy paranormal fascination that has gone viral in our society.

The problem is that the paranormal is a slippery slope and once an individual opens the door to the spirit (demonic) world, it only affects one's life negatively, and that door can be difficult to close. Do you, like the leaders from Issachar, understand the times we are living in? The results of comprehensive studies documenting the pervasive influence of paranormal phenomena are telling. A majority of Americans, 71 percent, claim they have personally had paranormal experiences; 37 percent believe in ghosts; 56 percent believe ghosts are spirits of the dead (see chapter 5 for my discussion of the widespread belief in Roman times that ghosts were the returned spirits of the wicked dead); and 37 percent believe that houses can be infiltrated and haunted by demonic spirits.[75]

Professors Christopher Bader, Carson Mencken, and Joseph Baker wrote *Paranormal America*, documenting their research on the paranormal fascination of Americans. The Baylor Religion Survey project was conducted in 2005 and 2007, and its associated results formed the basis for the conclusions in their book.[76] They discovered that "paranormal experiences are, in fact, surprisingly common in the United States."[77] Indeed, they confidently assert that 70–80 percent of Americans firmly believe in paranormal activity.[78]

Perhaps some people may think that paranormal fascination is something for uneducated people, but research says the opposite. Studies of undergraduate and graduate students point out that the more educated people are, the more likely they are to believe in the supernatural. For example, the University of Virginia recently launched a paranormal activity lab in which respected scientists are researching phenomena such as ESP, poltergeists, near death experiences (NDE), and out-of-body experiences.[79]

Research results of Americans from *Paranormal America*:[80]

- Almost one third of Americans have consulted their horoscope.
- Nearly 12 percent of Americans (or roughly 42 million people) have personally consulted a psychic, medium, or fortune-teller.
- Nearly 25 percent of Americans research ghosts and haunted houses (paranormal research).
- Nearly 25 percent of Americans are fascinated by UFO sightings, abductions, or tales of government UFO conspiracies.
- Nearly 21 percent of Americans believe in Big Foot and the Loch Ness Monster.

Therefore, I think we are asking the wrong question. The question is not whether or not you believe in the paranormal, because most people do, in one form or another. Rather, the question should be: What type of experience have you had with the paranormal? And more importantly, Why? Those who have had paranormal experiences are no longer thought of as strange or different. In many respects we are living in a world pervaded by the influence of spirits that is strikingly similar to the first-century world of Jesus.

The Paranormal Teaches a False Gospel, Makes Promises It Cannot Keep, and Will Always Drag People into Bondage and Confusion

Similar to Jesus of Nazareth, the apostle Paul had much to say about demonic activity. In 2 Corinthians 11:14, Paul warned that *"even Satan disguises himself as an angel of light."* Satan is the master deceiver who masquerades as an angel of light, a false beacon of hope. Hence the greater paranormal world can seem so "Christian." In my quest to answer the unanswered questions of spiritual darkness, I was struck by the Christian messaging of the paranormal world. Many Christians fall into the trap of these false promises. Mediums guarantee to help you unlock your purpose in life. Through their clairvoyance they claim that they will guide you through an unsure future. They will contact a dead loved one or friend so that you can say something to them or find necessary closure. Case in point, driving through my home city of Houston, I noticed an advertisement affixed to a psychic shop that promised "uniting lost lovers, even in death."

Unfortunately most people respond in a typically cynical way. A derisive response toward someone entrapped by the paranormal is unhelpful and even harmful. I have personally ministered to parents who have lost children. In those tender moments they have confessed to me that they would do absolutely anything to communicate with their dead child. Ergo, when someone experiences a loss combined with intense grief, they can be easily duped by such false promises. Stories are legion that confirm the paranormal world preys on the weakness of a grieving human disposition.

In another instance, a different psychic shop here in Houston generously promoted the fact that "your first two questions are free!" Most of the time we chuckle when we read these stories, wondering how on earth these people attract any business at all. With that mindset we overlook the fact that there is a hurting world around us. Mother's Day can be difficult if you've lost a mother, and the same goes with Father's Day. A friend of mine lost his son to suicide. Father's Day is a grim reminder of that for him. Christmas is the most difficult time of the year for many people who have lost dear family members. Many followers of Jesus are exploited by the paranormal "angels of light" when they are hurting. Therefore it should not surprise us at all that many people wandering through the fog of depression end up visiting a place that promises hope, albeit at a price.

Astonishingly, some psychics, mediums, and necromancers claim to be Christians in order to lure new clients. Over three hundred psychics, both male and female, claim to be ordained ministers, as well.[81] They advertise the fact that you are not consulting any ordinary medium but *an ordained medium*! According to the American Federation of Certified Psychics and

Mediums, 97 percent of psychics/mediums will not refund a customer for underwhelming results.[82] Perhaps that is why a significant number of mediums only use a first name or an alias. Even so, you might be surprised to learn that there are nearly twenty psychics in the United States who claim to be millionaires.[83]

In 1 John 4:1 we are challenged: *"Dear friends, do not believe every spirit, but test the spirits to see whether they are from God, because many false prophets have gone out into the world"* (NIV). The problem is that the majority of Christians lack discernment. They do not take this command seriously. Christianity has the most educated general membership in its history, but also the most undiscerning.

In 2006 David Kinnaman released a study highlighting the vulnerability of young people to the paranormal world. After surveying thousands of teenagers, the study found that 73 percent of teenagers have participated in contacting the dead and other related witchcraft activities beyond the more pedestrian exposure from entertainment channels or horoscopes. Four out of five teenagers have had their horoscopes read, "just for fun." The report also noted that a staggering seven million teenagers have "encountered an angel, demon, or some other supernatural being." Most notable to me was the fact that only 28 percent of our young people claimed they had learned anything at their church to help inform their views of the supernatural world.[84] No wonder the paranormal is a trending unanswered question in the church.

As a university professor, I visit other campuses from time to time to give lectures. In my travels I have been overwhelmed by the level of validation, even encouragement, given to all forms of paranormal expression on university campuses. This again proves the earlier point, that it is a myth to think the paranormal world is primarily attractive to uneducated people. You can visit universities today and attend campus-sponsored paranormal events: tarot card readings, palm readings, fortune-telling, even channeling—all promoted as harmless fun. So, on the one hand, we have this strange mixture of paranormal "entertainment" and on the other hand, a much deeper search from spiritual meaning—a search for meaning beyond our natural world. This is where millennials are today. God has been thrown off the campus. More and more professors are atheists, even nihilists, because they do not think there is anything to live for; life itself is seen a meaningless waste of time.

I am a professor at Houston Baptist University, an excellent Christian liberal arts university. That fact does not mean our students live in a utopia. One of my students scheduled an appointment with me to say that she had a "friend" who believed that life had no purpose or meaning and that she was planning to die at the age of thirty. Her "friend's" plan was to live wildly until her thirtieth birthday and then end her life. The false promise of the paranormal world rears its demonic head everywhere, even at a Christian university.

It does not matter what the atheist (or nihilist) professors claim. Human beings are spiritual beings. God's fingerprints are placed on every human heart. We hunger for the spiritual and when we've cast God out the door, when we ridicule and mock the Christian faith and replace it with odd, even diabolical, paranormal hocus pocus, we become entrapped. We believe in a false gospel. It is my experience from counseling hurting people that those who expose themselves to the paranormal world are more likely to be depressed, abuse others, commit crimes, and even attempt suicide.

It seems the devil reinvents himself in every generation. A generation ago it was the attraction of Satanism. Have you noticed that we rarely hear about Satanism anymore? It is a taboo subject. Seldom is the spooky word *occult* referenced in our society. Words like *Satanism* or *the occult* have gone out of fashion. *Paranormal* is now the trendy and acceptable term.

How do we apply the warning of 1 John 4:1? All believers must "*test the spirits*" by always comparing their experiences (and the paranormal messaging) with the Word of God. The paranormal expresses a message that there is no accountability for how we live our lives, that sin is not real, that there is no consequence in hell for sin and, therefore, no need for heaven, and that death is merely a transition to a more peaceful existence. When you get beyond the façade of the trendy terms, this is a message that has been around a long time. This false gospel was first presented in Genesis 3, when the serpent tempted Eve. As Christians we must be discerning. We are directed not to believe every spirit. Jesus said, "*And if I cast out demons by Beelzebul, by whom do your sons cast them out? Therefore they shall be your judges. But if it is by the finger of God that I cast out demons, then the kingdom of God has come upon you"* (Luke 11:19–20).

The expression *"finger of God"* brings to mind the confession of Pharaoh's magicians, namely, that the mighty works of Moses and Aaron were not from magic but from the *"finger of God"* (Exodus 8:19), that is, from God Himself. In Jewish tradition it was held that Pharaoh's magicians were empowered by Satan. Subsequently, Jesus' *"finger of God"* comment overlaps with the magician's confession and was compelling to His Jewish audience. Jesus has declared that His supernatural powers are not chicanery or empowered by the devil; Jesus' miracles are the result of His kingly power.[85] Moses warned against believing false signs and wonders:

> *If a prophet or a dreamer of dreams arises among you and gives you a sign or a wonder, and the sign or wonder that he tells you comes to pass, and if he says, 'Let us go after other gods,' which you have not known, 'and let us serve them,' you shall not listen to the words of that prophet or that dreamer of dreams. For the LORD your God is testing you, to know whether you love the LORD your God with all your heart and with all your soul. You shall walk after the LORD your God and fear him and keep his commandments and obey his voice, and you shall serve him and hold fast to him. But that prophet or that dreamer of dreams shall be put to death, because he has taught rebellion against the LORD your God, who brought you out of the land of Egypt and redeemed you out of the house of slavery, to make you leave the way in which the LORD your God commanded you to walk. So you shall purge the evil from your midst.* (Deuteronomy 13:1–5)

We should be challenged to follow the example of the Christians at Berea *"for they accepted the message most eagerly and studied the scriptures every day to see if what they were now being told were true"* (Acts 17:11 PHILLIPS). To Timothy, Paul said, *"Do not waste time arguing over godless ideas and old wives' tales. Instead, train yourself to be godly"* (1 Timothy 4:7 NLT).

Followers of Jesus are commanded by God's Word to avoid all interaction with the paranormal world. Stay away from it: *"Abstain from every form of evil"* (1 Thessalonians 5:22). There is nothing entertaining to God about the paranormal world. God's Word is clear: we are to avoid it. (See, for example, Deuteronomy 18:9–13.)

It is essential that parents are committed to listen, be attentive, and most importantly, be discerning about the activities of their children. (See chapters 8 and 10 for discussion on the importance of listening.) Parents are to be the guardians of their children, not only physically but spiritually, as well. If you or a family member have anything resembling paranormal paraphernalia in your possession, you should get rid of it immediately. This includes movies, music, photographs, clothing, books, Ouija boards, tarot cards, etc.

God worked a powerful revival in the city of Ephesus through the preaching of the apostle Paul. I have filmed in the massive theater (see Acts 19:29) on the Panayir Hill in Ephesus, which has the capacity to hold twenty-five thousand people. The acoustics are excellent. As a result of the gospel message being embraced *"a number of those who had practiced magic arts brought their books together and burned them in the sight of all. And they counted the value of them and found it came to fifty thousand pieces of silver"* (Acts 19:19). The value of their magical books (paranormal material) would have been valued in the range of six to seven million dollars today. After coming to faith, it was understood that these magical books had a corrosive impact on Ephesian culture and, therefore, they were discarded. We should follow this example.

Unfortunately, many Christians are not aware of their identity in Christ and the authority Jesus has imparted to them. Therefore, the unprepared believer lacks confidence not only to discuss the devil and demons, but also to overcome them. Paul understood what it was to engage with the devil: *"I fought with wild beasts at Ephesus"* (1 Corinthians 15:32). Yet Paul declared in his Ephesian letter that the believer has a powerful armament to defeat the devil: *"Finally, be strong in the Lord and in the strength of His might"* (Ephesians 6:10). As a Christian, your power and confidence to overcome the devil does not occur automatically. Notice the action words Paul uses in Ephesians 6:10–20: *"Put on the full armor of God"* (verse 11); *"take up the full armor of God"* (verse 13); *"stand firm therefore, HAVING GIRDED YOUR LOINS WITH TRUTH"* (verse 14 NASB, also a reference to Isaiah 11:5); *"taking up the shield of faith"* (verse 16 NASB); *"and take the HELMET*

OF *SALVATION*" (verse 17 NASB, another reference to Isaiah 59:17). These action words describe the continual work of the believer to overcome the enemy when he strikes—and strike he will. The implication of Paul's language in Ephesians 6 is that we are an active agent, not a passive observer, in battling the enemy. In the next chapter we will explore the authority of the believer in Jesus, as well as the fact that Jesus alone imparts truth, brings freedom, reveals our ultimate purpose, and offers lasting peace.

12

HE WHO IS IN ME IS GREATER THAN HE WHO IS IN THE WORLD

C. S. Lewis (1898–1963) emerged as a celebrity in North America with the 1942 release of his wartime bestseller, *The Screwtape Letters,* a book he dedicated to his dear friend, J. R. R. Tolkien. *The Screwtape Letters,* thirty-one in number, originally appeared in a series of articles published in a church magazine called *The Guardian.*[86] The letters were so popular that a year after their appearance in *The Guardian,* they were published as a small book for a wider popular audience. Alister McGrath noted that Tolkien was not all that pleased to have such a lowbrow popular book dedicated to him.[87] In any case, *The Screwtape Let-*

ters challenged the mind and stretched the heart as few books did during World War II, and the fact that the book was relatively short made it accessible to a large audience. In the preface, Lewis drew a timeless comparison about two wrong attitudes related to the devil—a comparison perhaps even more relevant today:

> There are two equal and opposite errors into which our race can fall about the devils. One is to disbelieve in their existence. The other is to believe, and to feel an excessive and unhealthy interest in them.[88]

As you contemplate Lewis's statement, how would you evaluate your perception and attitude towards spiritual darkness? In *A Tale of Two Cities,* Charles Dickens described the era: "It was the best of times, it was the worst of times, it was the age of wisdom, it was the age of foolishness, it was the epoch of belief, it was the epoch of incredulity, it was the season of Light, it was the season of Darkness, it was the spring of hope, it was the winter of despair."

As we saw in chapter 6, life expectancy today is at an all-time high in many parts of the industrialized world, and yet globally, more people are enslaved today than ever before. In many ways we are living in a time of great advances, yet lurking behind the veil of this world is a real devil whose demons prey on the mind and body, which is evidenced by the current mayhem throughout society.

The legendary Bible teacher Warren Wiersbe once said, "The Christian life is not a playground; it is a battleground." This sounds good in a Bible study setting, but it is difficult to live out. The problem with this statement is that most followers of Jesus are not ready for battle with *"this dark world"* (Ephesians 6:12 NLT). We learn more about the devil and demons from the four Gospels than from any other part of the Bible. Demons can cause illness (see Matthew 10:1; 12:2; 17:15–18), agony (see Mathew 15:22), loss of ability to speak (see Matthew 9:32), and pain (see Luke 6:18; Matthew 17:15). *Demon,* which is translated from the Greek *daimōn,* is not the exclusive name for Satan's minions. Since there is no Hebrew word for *demon,* the gospels frequently make use of the Old Testament words for an "unclean" or "evil" spirit. For example, King Saul was tormented several times by an *"evil spirit"* (1 Samuel 16:14–16; 18:10; 19:9 NIV).

It is noteworthy that the plural form *"demons"* (Greek: *daimonion*) is used sixty-three times in the New Testament (fifty-three of which are in the Gospels), far more than the singular form. The modern terms "demon-possessed" or "demon possession" do not occur in the Greek New Testament. In the original we never read of a demon "possessing" another person. The proper terminology for having a demon or being controlled by a demon is to be "demonized" (*daimonizomai*), derived from Matthew 4:24; 8:16, 28, 33; 9:32; 12:22; 15:22; Mark 1:32; 5:15–16, 18; Luke 8:36; and John 10:21. Merrill Unger described the abilities of demons this way: "As spiritual beings, demons are intelligent, vicious, unclean, with power to afflict men with physical hurt, and moral and spiritual contamination."[89] The content of this definition is taken from the Gospels, where demonic activity is shown to be normative in society. (See, for example, James 2:19; Luke 4:33–34; 9:43; Matthew 25:41.)

An Epic Battle: The Kingdom of Jesus Versus the Kingdom of Satan

The central aim of Jesus' mission was preaching the establishment of the kingdom of God: *"From that time Jesus began to preach, saying, 'Repent, for the kingdom of heaven is at hand'"* (Matthew 4:17). Indeed, the kingdom of God is inseparably linked to the gospel, or the Good News, for which Israel and the world has waited: *"The time is fulfilled, and the kingdom of God is at hand; repent and believe in the gospel"* (Mark 1:15). A striking yet more often than not overlooked feature in Jesus' preaching was His inseparable link of the kingdom of God with exorcism. Exorcism was not a sidebar issue in Jesus' ministry, rather it was a feature. Exorcism is emblematic and, in fact, evidences the destruction of Satan and the power of Jesus. Jesus said that Satan's kingdom was on a mission to deceive, destroy, and even kill: *"You are of your father the devil, and your will is to do your father's desires. He was a murderer from the beginning, and does not stand in the truth, because there is no truth in him. When he lies, he speaks out of his own character, for he is a liar and the father of lies*" (John 8:44). Satan will lie to you. He will corrupt the truth.

Most of us recall moments when we have believed the lies of the devil. Satan's mission is to bring confusion into our lives. A few verses earlier, Jesus was speaking to His followers, saying that because they knew Jesus, "*you will know the truth and the truth will make you free*" (John 8:32 NASB). Some of you reading this need to be set free from the bondage and confusion of Satan. Jesus will set you free. Jesus said, "*I am the light of the world. Whoever follows me will not walk in darkness, but will have the light of life*" (John 8:12). "*The thief comes only to steal and kill and destroy. I came that they may have life and have it abundantly*" (John 10:10). Do you know the truth? Are you in the truth? Or are you in the clutches of confusion?

Throughout Jesus' ministry He engaged demons and unclean spirits. Similar to the popularity of the paranormal in our time, exorcism was big business in the first century. One could make a fine living as a professional exorcist in Roman times. Unfortunately, in Acts 19, we see firsthand what happens when you are unprepared to encounter a demon: "*And the man in whom was the evil spirit leaped on them and subdued all of them and overpowered them, so that they fled out of that house naked and wounded*" (Acts 19:16 NASB). It is important to notice that the text states these Jewish exorcists were traveling professionals "*who went from place to place*" (verse 13 NASB).

Luke offers an interesting layer of detail noting that the humiliated professional exorcists were overpowered and left the demonic encounter naked. Similar to the uniforms worn today by professional sports teams, exorcists in the first century were adorned with special apparel thought to enhance their influence over the dark spirit world. The fame and power of Jesus' name had evidently spread so fast and far that Jewish exorcists were happy to use His name, the implication being that these Jews were using the name of Jesus professionally but had no allegiance to Him personally. It did not matter that Jewish exorcists were armored like ancient ghostbusters or warlocks, because they were unprepared and utterly defeated.

By contrast, Jesus' power was such that He defeated demons with a single word: "*That evening they brought to him many who were oppressed by demons, and he cast out the spirits with a word and healed all who were sick*" (Matthew 8:16). Jesus appointed twelve apostles (literally "ones sent") to "*preach and have authority to cast out demons*" (Mark 3:14–15). "*They went out and proclaimed....And they cast out many demons*" (Mark 6:12, 13). In Luke the linkage between proclaiming gospel of the kingdom of God and exorcism is emphasized: "*And he called the twelve together and gave them power and authority over all demons and to cure diseases, and he sent them out to proclaim the kingdom of God and to heal....And they departed and went through the villages, preaching the gospel and healing everywhere*" (Luke 9:1–2, 6).

In Mark 1:24 Jesus is confronted by a spirit: "*What have you to do with us, Jesus of Nazareth? Have you come to destroy us? I know who you are—the Holy One of God.*" Jesus' response was to immediately silence and cast out the unclean spirit. Notice from the passage that Jesus' dominance over the demon was so dramatic that the crowd cried out: "*What is this? A new teaching with authority! He commands even the unclean spirits, and they obey Him*" (Mark 1:27 NASB).

The name of Jesus was so powerful that He had the ability to cast out demons from long distance. From Mark 7:24–30 we learn that the mother returned home to discover that the demon had left her daughter and she had been completely healed. Jesus' power over demons was so remarkable that of Him it was said, "*Nothing like this has ever been seen in Israel!*" (Matthew 9:33). This is why the crowds around Him pressed in on Him and, in Matthew, we hear the cry of the afflicted woman, "*If I only touch his garment, I will be made well*" (Matthew 9:21).

The New Testament attests that the name of Jesus is mighty and powerful. Setting people free from the bondage of demonic activity characterized His ministry then, and it remains the case today. The mission of Jesus is to usher in the kingdom of heaven on earth. His exorcisms and healings are tangible evidence of the presence of His kingdom ministry. Jesus dismantled Satan's kingdom. Jesus proclaimed, "*If a kingdom is divided against itself, that kingdom cannot stand. And if a house is divided against itself, that house cannot stand. And if Satan has risen up against himself, and is divided, he cannot stand, but has an end*" (Mark 3:24–26 NKJV). The reference to the divided kingdom implies that Jesus views Satan's sphere of power as a kingdom, a kingdom at war with the kingdom of God. The last part of the quotation is *"has an end"* (*telos echei* in Greek). Therefore, Satan's sphere is being weakened. He was the strong one but a stronger One is here now. Satan's house will not stand. (See, for example, Matthew 12, Mark 3:27, Luke 11:21–22.) Satan is in retreat mode today. He is powerless against Christ and has no authority over a follower of Jesus. A Christian has nothing to fear of the demonic paranormal world. When I understand my identity in Christ, there is freedom from bondage. This is why John wrote in his epistle, *"for he who is in you is greater than he who is in the world"* (1 John 4:4).

One of the most spiritually stimulating books in my library is the three-volume seventeenth-century work *The Christian in Complete Armour* by William Gurnall. John Newton, the author of "Amazing Grace," was known for saying that if he could only read one book beside the Bible, it would be *The Christian in Complete Armour,* such was its influence over him. Charles Spurgeon said that Gurnall's book would renew his spirit: "I have often resorted to it when my own fire has been burning low, and I have seldom failed to find a glowing coal upon Gurnall's hearth."[90] My favorite Gurnall-ism is found in volume one of his series: "Unbelief fears Satan as a lion, faith treads upon him as a worm."[91] Do you fear Satan as a lion? Or are you strengthened in faith so that you can bulldoze Satan like a worm?

Gurnall's question challenges the heart:

> Thus the Christian, when he comes to the pinch indeed, is able, through Christ, to trample Satan under his feet; yet before the conflict, stands trembling at the thought of him....Abundant provision is made against [Satan's] assaults. The saint is wrapped up in the everlasting arms of almighty power, and what can a cursed devil do against God, who laid those chains on him which he cannot shake off?[92]

Always remember that Jesus said *"all authority"* is His and He will be with us *"until the end of the world"* (Matthew 28:18, 20).

13

ENGAGEMENT PRINCIPLE #3: BE COOL, THOUGHT LEADER

Be cool, thought leader. Yes, I am addressing to you. Thought leadership is a trendy new description of an individual who owns his or her field of expertise. Being a thought leader is not a pejorative term that means your thoughts are better than the thoughts of others, either. A thought leader is an authority—useful, knowledgeable, fresh, and most of all, able to project strength by communicating with calmness. A thought leader disarms his or her audience. A thought leader studies, is committed to improvement, and invests time with other thought leaders. Of course, Jesus was quintessentially a thought leader. His ideas have impacted the world unlike anyone else. God has called *every* believer to be a "faith thought leader," not only a select few. Paul told Timothy that he needed to be a thought leader: "*Do your best to present yourself to God as one approved, a worker who has no need to be ashamed, rightly handling the word of truth*" (2 Timothy 2:15). "*Do your best,*" in English, derives from a single Greek word: *spoudázō*. This word can also be translated as "be eager," "to hurry," "make every effort," and to act with "intensity."

Far too many Christians are not thought leaders. They are lazy about their faith. They feel no urgency. When they prepare for a faith conversation, it can be as if they were preparing for war: *Attack!* This is the exact opposite of what we see modeled in the life of Christ. The truth is *comforting,* meaning the more you know, the more relaxed you'll be. As a professor I can attest to this point. I can usually make an educated guess as to which students in my courses will do well on their finals by watching their body language. Students who apply themselves to the course material are generally more relaxed than the students who are unprepared. As you prepare to answer complex questions about your faith, you must know that, in large part, you are entering an academic contest. It is a contest in the world of thinking, and you do not go into that contest unprepared. The questions we are addressing in *Unanswered* are taken very seriously, both inside and outside the church. The content deserves our best effort, because it brings transformation to peoples' lives. We need to strengthen our ability to conduct comfortable and effective faith conversations, not debate or battle but succinctly and confidently share why Jesus is the Hope in which we believe.

One of the purposes for this study is to provide you with more understanding and knowledge about your faith. When you have tools and answers like those presented in this book, you will not need to retreat or shy away from tackling tough questions. You can relax and confidently stand up for the truth of God's Word. We need you. We need people committed to the vision of communicating the case for their faith, not only at the community level but at the highest academic level. This is why I have dedicated my life to training Christian thinkers.

I'll never forget the day I received this question at Christian Thinkers Society: "A 'Christian-Thinker'—isn't that an oxymoron?" Honestly, for many Christians it *is* an oxymoron. Skeptics reason that describing followers of Jesus as "thinkers" is similar to saying something self-contradicting, like "cruel kindness" or a "new classic." Many skeptics have never encountered a Christian thinker and are unable to make sense of it. We can and should do better. Jesus said that the greatest commandment was to *"love the Lord your God with all your heart and with all your soul and with* ***all your mind"*** (Matthew 22:37).

It is an exciting time to be a Christian but it is also a more difficult time. Therefore, another important discipline we need to adopt is to spend more time reading, studying, and meditating on Scripture. Commit yourself to watching less television, reducing time spent on Facebook, and devoting more time to reading and improving yourself. When you come to the end of your life you will not wish you had spent more time aimlessly scrolling your Facebook newsfeed. You will wish you had invested more time with Jesus in God's Word, *"in whom are hidden all the treasures of wisdom and knowledge"* (Colossians 2:3). As you gain confidence and learn to answer the unanswered questions, this will cause your approach in witnessing to be far more relaxed; dare I even say, you will appear "cool." Certainly, you will project peace as you confidently and calmly make your case for faith. I hope you will leave this chapter deeply committed to love the Lord with your mind, offering your very best as a Christian thought leader.

PART 5

BIBLE-ISH CHRISTIANITY: WHY MOST CHRISTIANS KNOW JUST ENOUGH ABOUT THE BIBLE TO BE DANGEROUS

14

THE BEST-SELLING BOOK OF ALL TIME THAT FEW READ AND FEWER UNDERSTAND

Americans spend nearly 2.5 billion dollars a year on Bibles and related Christian materials (it has been estimated Americans spend a half-billion dollars per year buying new Bibles[93]—and that number is increasing[94]). This reality brings to mind the thoughts of Samuel Clemens (aka, Mark Twain), who once remarked, "'Classic.' A book which people praise and don't read." This is an unprecedented time in modern Christianity, and Western society in general, as is it relates to the intersection of the life of the mind with the authority for faith. For perhaps the first time in history, there is a burgeoning Christian community attempting a faith that is, for the most part, absent of the Bible, and there are secularists who desire a "bible" without reference to God. To be sure, some Christians flaunt the fact that their faith has little to no recourse to the Bible, but a careful evaluation of the content of their faith betrays them. Attempting to be a Christian without the Bible is no different from attempting to strengthen your body by depriving yourself of nutrition and sleep. Yet this is the reality of a growing swath of churches across North America, in both small churches and megachurches. I refer to this trend as "Bible-*ish*" Christianity, or perhaps, more pejoratively, *knowing just enough about the Bible to be dangerous*. What will happen when the anchor that has united the Christian faith for two millennia across all denominations—the Bible—is cast aside? Heretofore, the beauty and attraction of Christianity has been its community, united not only in Christ but also in their use of the same Book.

Bible-less Christianity, the Declining Influence of the Bible in America

The Bible has become a moving target in our day in age. One can strip it down, twist it, misread it, add to it, supplement it, and even overrule it, and, unfortunately, 95 percent of the congregation will not even realize it. Why? Because they do not know the Bible. There was a time when Christians carried their Bibles to church with them. One of the most worshipful sounds I remember hearing in the church was when the pastor encouraged the congregation to "turn in your Bibles to (such and such a passage)," followed by the rushing sound of shifting pages fluttering throughout the auditorium. I rarely hear this sound anymore. Of course, electronic Bible resources have in some sense replaced the sound of the page (although this is contested as more adults said they used a printed version of the Bible in 2015 than in 2014[95]), but few would argue the fact that today only a minority of Christians are committed to bringing the Scriptures to church with them. And why would they? Will the sermon even reference the Bible? Perhaps the sermon will grab some passages here or there and foist them together, at best.

Meanwhile, while some Christians are minimizing the Bible, other communities are happy to use it—kind of—albeit with slight modification. Professor A. C. Grayling published *The Good Book: A Humanist Bible* in 2011.[96] This "bible" is unique in that it is completely secular. It contains no mention of God or the gospel, and certainly no reference to sin. It is billed and touted as "the Bible for philosophers." A compilation of wisdom inspired by thinkers like Cicero, Confucius, and Herodotus replaces the Man upstairs, with His rather outdated thinking. The jacket copy reveals that this book is exactly what society needs: "For a secular age in which many find that religion no longer speaks to them, *The Good Book* is a literary tour de force—a book of life and practice invoking the greatest minds of the past in the perennial challenge of being human."[97] *The Good Book* "invokes" the greatest minds of the past, but oddly enough, Jesus is never discussed—that is, the historical Jesus.

Bible-ish Christianity

Western Christianity is best defined as Bible-*ish*. Adding the suffix "-ish" is intentional because *-ish* has evolved into a term of its own. *Ish* means "kind of, sort of, somewhat," and first appeared as a word in 2003 in the online, crowdsourced *Urban Dictionary*, and it has enjoyed a wider acceptance since then. The evidence is overpowering that contemporary Christianity is Bible-*ish*, at best, and, at worst, and in some cases, Bible-*less*.

Today's church is malnourished. Christians are biblically illiterate and theologically shallow, which has led to the tragic consequence of mass deconversion across all denominations. If we cannot explain the power of the gospel as it is revealed in the Bible, why would we expect anything different from what we see trending today? In my courses at Houston Baptist University, I was recently teaching a Bible survey class to first- and second-year undergraduate students. Most of the thirty-six students would self-identify as followers of Jesus, however, only three out of the thirty-six said they had ever *read* the entire Bible. None of them said they had read the Bible with any systemic regularity. If you were in my position and had to explain the long story of the Bible to an audience who had never read it, what would you say?

What is the Bible? Where did it come from? Was it overnighted from heaven on golden tablets? Who wrote it? Is the Bible different from other holy books, and if so, how? What is the story of the Bible, anyway? Why was the Bible written? When was it written? How can we be certain it is authoritative from beginning to end? Are there errors in the Bible? Why do some Bibles have additional books that are not in my copy?

Unfortunately, few Christians possess enough confidence in their own understanding of the Bible to answer these rather pedestrian questions. Hence a new demographic now flourishes: the "ex-Christian." The most spiritually fragile age group, people between the ages of eighteen and thirty-four, are abandoning the faith at alarming levels. The "unchurched" are now more popularly referred to as the "Nones" (forty-six million and growing), people who know almost nothing of the Bible's basic content and core message of redemption. The American Bible Society releases an annual report, the latest one called *State of the Bible 2015*, and their findings are helpful in our discussion. Additional recent studies out of Canada and the United Kingdom provide an updated perspective on the declining influence of the Bible across the West:

- Twenty-five million copies of the Bible are sold annually.
- Almost 80 percent of Americans "believe the Bible is the Word of God."[98]
- Nearly half of the Christians in America say they are too busy to read the Bible.[99]
- Just one in four Americans can correctly identify that *"the truth will set you free"* (John 8:32) is the only statement found in the Bible among a list of four options.[100]
- More than one-third of adults believe the statement "God works in mysterious ways" is found in the Bible.[101] (See chapter 9, this is a statement from William Cowper.)

- The average American household owns 4.4 Bibles (or somewhere between 3 and 10).[102]
- Eighty-eight percent of Americans own one at least one Bible.[103]
- Just one in seven adults say they read the Bible daily.[104]
- One in four adults say they never read the Bible.[105]
- Just 12 percent of adults rate themselves as highly knowledgeable of the Bible.[106]
- Thirty-three percent of millennials admit never reading the Bible and are more likely than any other adult generation to have a skeptical attitude toward Scripture.[107]
- Nineteen percent of Americans say the Bible has too much influence in society.[108]
- Seventy-two percent of Americans believe incorrectly that the Bible is available in all languages; however, over 50 percent of the world's languages still do not have a Bible translation.[109]
- Forty-seven percent of Canadian youth have never been inside a church facility.[110]
- One-third of British parents recently surveyed thought that Harry Potter was a thematic plotline derived from the Bible.[111]
- Three out of ten British children have no understanding of the Bible.[112]

Recently I attended a church growth conference in Atlanta at which a well-known evangelical pastor said to the room of four thousand church leaders, "I do not preach the Bible verse-by-verse, because that is boring." I would not have believed it had I not been present when these words were spoken. Though his name is not important for the point I am making in this study, I obviously respected this pastor and his outreach to greater Atlanta enough to go to the expense of going to the conference to learn from him and his team. I left disheartened. The subtle message was that if you want to grow your church, become more like Disney and downplay the Bible; at least that was the message I heard. Why not be more like Disney centered on the Bible? That is for another book. The point stands. We live in a time of increasing biblical illiteracy, even among our church leaders. The Bible is rarely referenced by many of the popular television preachers. Consequently, I fear we are one generation away from a major heretical schism in the church.

The Bible is not held in the esteem it once was. Over the last one hundred fifty years, America has drifted away from its focus on the Bible. For example, though he was not a member of any church, the Bible was valued as an authority in America so much so that Abraham Lincoln quoted from it four strategic times in his second inaugural address on March 4, 1865. President Lincoln used words ascribed to Jesus from Matthew 18:7 and pronounced God's judgment on our nation for her moral bankruptcy of slavery:

> "*Woe unto the world because of offenses! for it must needs be that offenses come; but woe to that man by whom the offense cometh!*" If we shall suppose that American slavery is one of those offenses which, in the providence of God, must needs come, but which, having continued through His appointed time, He now wills to remove, and that He gives to both North and South this terrible war as the woe due to those by whom the offense came, shall we discern therein any departure from those divine attributes which the believers in a living God always ascribe to Him? Fondly do we hope, fervently do we pray, that this mighty scourge of war may speedily pass away.[113]

Professor Mark Noll has convincingly shown that after the passage of only a decade after the Civil War (1865–1875), America's biblical foundation was cracking, beginning an irreversible decline that has extended to this present day.[114] Emblematic of the Bible's declining influence is what Harper Lee wrote of in chapter 5 of her 1960 novel *To Kill a Mockingbird*, in which the character Miss Maudie says, "Sometimes the Bible in the hand of one man is worse than a whiskey bottle in the hand of [another]." Clearly, the challenge of biblical illiteracy in America is not because of a shortage of Bibles, but rather knowledge and appreciation of the Bible's message.

The Bible in Klingon (*Star Trek*)

My wife, Audrey, has a hobby that I quite enjoy—healthy cooking! She is talented at creating new healthy recipes. I've even done my best to have a hand in this new found love of cooking by encouraging her to start a Christian food blog! We enjoy learning more about cooking and the variety of cuisine available in different cultures. This hobby started out of necessity as we came to realize that there is a dreadful correlation with being involved in Christian ministry and gaining weight, so we made a commitment nearly ten years ago to begin a healthy lifestyle. This necessitated that we invest time and resources into learning more about appropriate nutrition and healthy eating habits. It has been a successful endeavor. We enjoy our new lifestyle and no longer refer to it as a "diet." In our quest to increase our knowledge of healthy meals we began watching cooking shows, visiting cooking stores, and reading about ways to enjoy good food while not increasing our waistlines. We were watching Fox News recently and the host pointed out that we have more cooking programs, more cooking shows, more cookbooks, and cook blogs, and yet, the statistics show that, for the first time ever, more people are eating out![115] Americans now spend more on dining out than on eating in their own homes.

This new trend made me think of the correlation of the Bible in American society. Bibles have never been more affordable or accessible than they are today. We have more Bible translations, more study aids, and more devotionals—our bookstores are flooded with Christian resources—but for all of these available tools, Americans are reading and studying the Bible less.

The unwillingness of many Americans to dig deeper into the Scriptures is not related to a lack of options. The Gideons give away a Bible every second of every day. One Christian publisher currently sells more than sixty different editions of the Bible. This publisher has provided an "all seasons Bible," a "skater's Bible," a "surfer's Bible," a "cowboy Bible, a "stay-at-home mom Bible," and for the kiddos, they even sell the "super heroes' Bible." There is a Bible available for people who are too busy to read the Bible: *The 100-Minute Bible*. You can learn everything you need to know about the Bible in less than two hours (wink, wink). Earlier I noted that the majority of Americans wrongly think the Bible is available in all languages. Well, never mind the fact that half of the world's languages do not have a Bible translation! Who needs earth when the Bible has been translated into Klingon, the fictitious alien language on *Star Trek*.

Martin Luther Might Roll Over in His Grave

The miracle of the preservation of the Bible is one of the strongest evidences for the veracity of Scripture. Have you stopped to consider how phenomenal it is that anything from the Christian past has survived at all? For a real-time example, the Islamic State (ISIS or ISIL) has been destroying antiquities in the Middle East. Statues from the classical period have been demolished, some dating to the seventh century BC.[116] ISIS has burned books and priceless ancient manuscripts. These tragedies are occurring in our sophisticated, modern era. The Christian church was terrorized for the first three hundred years of its existence. The fact that we have any early Christian documents at all is a miracle. By comparison, Herod the Great (c. 74–4 BC) had a secretary named Nicholas of Damascus, who wrote a universal history of the ancient world in 144 volumes. It has been completely lost to history. None of it survives.[117]

There was a time in my life when I did not know the story of how we got the Bible. This gap in my knowledge led to an overall sense of indifference towards it. When I was a teenager my father encouraged me to drill down further, not only to learn the Bible text but also to gain appreciation for the fact that we even *had* an English Bible. Once you learn the story of the Bible's preservation, the cost that was involved—and it was a terrible cost—you will never again open the Scriptures with the same detached, careless attitude. The story of how the Bible has come down to us is a tale of heroism, courage, persecution, betrayal, and towering faith in a God who raises the dead, mixed, through the centuries, with the blood of many martyrs. When Paul wrote to Timothy, he admonished him to be fervently committed to the Word of God: *"and that from childhood you have known the Holy Scriptures, which are able to make you wise for salvation through faith which is in Christ Jesus"* (2 Timothy 3:15 NKJV). This is the purpose of the Bible, to bring you into a relationship with the living God through His

Son, Jesus Christ, our Lord. And yet, there was a time (*c.* AD 1408) when to possess a copy of the Bible in England was a crime punishable by death. The Bible was a lost book to the people then, much as it is today; but in their day it was a question of access, not of apathy, as it is today.

There I stood in the room of the German friar, Martin Luther, where, lore has it, he flung his ink well at the devil and it crashed against the wall. The wall has now been stripped bare to the framing. Over the centuries, visitors to the Wartburg Castle, outside of Eisenach, Germany, have availed themselves of pieces of this famous wall as a memento of Luther's fight with the devil during his isolation and Bible translation work. Luther risked his life to make the Scriptures available to the German people in their native tongue so that they would easily understand it. At the age of thirty-three he boldly condemned the injustices of the Catholic Church's sale of indulgences by nailing the Ninety-Five Theses to the church door in Wittenberg, an act that thrust him to the forefront as the leader of the Protestant Reformation.[118] I later visited the birthplace of the Dominican, Johann Tetzel, who famously wrote, "As soon as a coin in the coffer rings, the soul from purgatory springs," in his quest to raise money for the construction of St. Peter's Basilica. In any case, on April 18, 1521, Luther appeared before the imperial diet (congress) at Worms and refused to recant his accusation, aligning himself in opposition to an empire and the Catholic Church. Luther said, "I am bound to the Scriptures I have quoted and my conscience is captive to the Word of God. I cannot and I will not retract anything, since it is neither safe nor right to go against conscience! Here I stand; I cannot do otherwise, so help me God! Amen."[119]

Charles V, ruler of both the Holy Roman Empire and the Spanish Empire, placed Luther under an imperial ban—essentially an empire-wide kill order. At Luther House in Wittenberg, I read the edict of Worms from Charles V:

> We strictly order that...you shall refuse to give Martin Luther hospitality, lodging, food, or drink; neither shall anyone, by word or deed, security or openly, succour or assist him by counsel or help; but in whatever place you meet him, you shall take him prisoner and...you shall deliver him, or cause him to be delivered, to us

> or at least let us now where he may be captured....Consequently, we command you, each and all...that henceforth no one shall dare to buy, sell, read, preserve, copy, print, or cause to be copied or printed, any books of the aforesaid Martin Luther.[120]

On May 4, 1521, Luther's longtime supporter and friend with means, Frederick the Wise, arranged for him to be abducted on his journey home from Worms and hidden away in one of the thirteen castles he owned. In the Thuringia forest, friendly raiders on horseback and armed with cross-bows captured Luther, blindfolded him, and delivered him to Wartburg Castle, no doubt saving the outlaw. Luther had to conceal his identity and take on the assumed name Junker Jörg (Knight George) and reside in the seclusion of Wartburg Castle for nearly a year (May 1521–March 1522). At one point Luther was forced to dress as a woman to evade identification.

Luther used the time to study and write extensively. Religious scholar Martin Marty adds that "Luther wrote more in his ten months cooped up in the castle than most scholars could in ten years."[121] For the first time in history, Luther translated the New Testament from the original Greek into German, a feat he accomplished in eleven weeks. Since Wartburg Castle is situated atop a 600-foot ridge, several Luther historians believe this inspired him to write the hymn "A Mighty Fortress Is Our God." First published in 1529, no copies of the first edition survive. Luther House has the only known copy of the second edition, printed in 1533. Notwithstanding an empire-wide kill order against him, Luther courageously produced a German Bible fully accessible to all in the common tongue. Luther's Bible had a profound influence in Germany and codified the modern German language as we know and appreciate it today.

In Luther House, Luther's approach to Scripture is memorialized: "The gospel is so clear that it does not need a great deal of interpretation, but it wants to be carefully looked at and deeply taken to heart." Harold Rawlings notes the far reaching magnitude of Luther's New Testament translation: "The appearance of Luther's New Testament in 1522 remains one of the most noteworthy and far-reaching events in the history of the Christian world, indeed, in the history of the world. His Bible introduced mass media, unified a nation, and set the standard for future translations."[122]

Luther's mission was based on his belief in *sola scriptura* (only Scripture), that the Bible alone was the final authority for the Christian faith, not church tradition. This view required Luther to produce a Bible understood by all Germans.

Luther would turn over in his grave if he experienced the Bible-*ish* Christianity of today. Luther's story of courage in the face of exile, oppression, and persecution inspires us to appreciate the Bible. We have so many diversions today that impede our spiritual growth and distract us from studying God's Word. We need to turn the tide and return to the Bible as *sola scriptura,* which means we should show the Scriptures respect by investing our time into knowing them better. For Luther, the study of the Bible was his central focus, not a sidebar issue—a Bible-centric approach to Christianity:

> For some years now I have read through the Bible twice every year. If you picture the Bible to be a mighty tree and every word a little branch, I have shaken every one of these branches because I wanted to know what it was and what it meant.[123]

In *Leadership Is an Art,* Max DePree writes, "The first job of a leader is to accurately describe reality."[124] As Christians we need to understand the reality of biblical illiteracy, first in our own lives and families but also in the church. Then we must collectively ask God for a revival of interest and commitment to the Holy Scriptures. In our next chapter we will discuss why the Bible is not only a Book to know, more than that, it is a Book to be experienced.

15

UNTIL HEAVEN AND EARTH PASS AWAY: REFORMING A BIBLE-ISH CHRISTIANITY

It seems that everyone has an opinion about the Bible. Politicians attempt to use it; Grammy Award-winners quote it; Hollywood has portrayed it on the big screen; and yet, one problem remains: most people are oblivious to the Bible's basic content, meaning, and core message. We say we believe in the Bible. We say we regard it as inspired and authoritative. We say that we agree with the historic stance of the church that the Scriptures infallibly communicate God's truth, because it is His

Word. If this is the case, we should show the Bible some respect by knowing more about it.

In 2015 I wrote *Jesus and the Jihadis* with Professor Craig Evans, assessing the threat posed by ISIS (also known as the Islamic State or ISIL). A byproduct of my research was an appreciation for the title *hafiz* (male), or *hafiza* (female), which means "guardian" in Arabic. In Islam, the hafiz is revered above all others, because that individual has memorized, with the ability to recite all 114 Arabic Suras, the 600-page Qur'an. In 2015 President Obama appointed a hafiz, Rashad Hussain, to lead the Center for Strategic Counterterrorism Communications. Fewer than 20 percent of the world's 1.5 billion Muslims speak Arabic. This fact does not stop Muslims from attempting to memorize the Arabic Qur'an. They might not understand the Arabic words, but they certainly can recite them. There are thousands of Muslim youth, sleeping on the floors of madrassas (Islamic schools) across Muslim lands studying to become a hafiz. The majority of Christians do not know how the Qur'an compares to the Bible and they do not realize the Qur'an proper (not including the Haditha or Sira) is actually smaller than the New Testament. Nonetheless, if the fact that Muslim youth are committed to memorizing their holy book in a language they do not understand does not convict you, you should check your pulse. I think we can do better as a church. Certainly we can offer God more investment in the Scriptures and stop giving Him the leftovers, here or there.

The Bible: Holy Survivor

Government-sponsored destruction of the Bible has occurred for two thousand years. Even in the English-speaking world, significant attempts have been made to usher the Bible into extinction. After John Wycliffe (1320–1384) and his followers created an uproar by translating the Latin Bible (Latin died as a language with the Roman Empire in AD 476) into English, it became a capital offense to translate, read, or possess an English Bible. In the fall of 1526, the Bishop of London, Cuthbert Tunstall, led a massive book burning behind St. Paul's Cathedral, in an area known as St. Paul's Cross.[125] Thousands of Bibles were lost, including precious Tyndale New Testaments.

Throughout the first three centuries of the church, the Roman government unleashed a fury on Christianity that has was more sporadic and spontaneous rather than sustained or uninterrupted. During the reigns of Nero (54–68) and Vespasian (69–79), Christians were fiercely persecuted. Unparalleled in his brutality against Christians, the infamous Emperor Diocletian (284–305) issued an edict in 303 to destroy all Christian books and buildings. Enduring torture and death, many Christians died with their sacred writings because of their unwillingness to hand over their Scriptures to the imperial authority. Even so, according to the Institute for New Testament Textual Research in Munster, Germany, we have 5,805 Greek manuscripts of the New Testament that predate the printing press. Remarkably, more than fifty of these ancient manuscripts date back to before the year 300, which is astounding considering the aforementioned persecutions. My friend and colleague, Craig Evans, recently made global headlines when he revealed that we might have a first-century fragment from the gospel of Mark, found in a mummy mask, although we cannot say this for sure as the study has not been released.[126] The small fragment of the gospel of Mark might even date to the first century. Compared to the manuscripts of classical Greece and Rome, the New Testament evidence is quite substantial.

During my doctoral residency at Oxford, I made it my personal ambition to invest as much time as I could studying the oldest and most valuable manuscripts of the Bible. I have had the enriching and humbling experience of holding the oldest, most priceless biblical fragments and manuscripts with my own hands. Evans, also my doctoral advisor, surprised me when said that he thought I had held more biblical manuscripts in my hands than 90 percent of Bible scholars. I am in love with the Word of God. Each fragment has a story of discovery and preservation. I made the trek from Oxford to the University of Manchester and studied the famous St. John's Fragment at the John Rylands Library. It is known as P52—that is, Papyrus 52—and it has the distinction of being the oldest fragment of the New Testament, dating to AD 125. What is remarkable about P52 is that the original, the autograph of the gospel of John, was written only 25–30 years before P52, which means they were circulating at the same time! The fragment is only 2.5 by 3.5 inches but it contains seven lines on both sides (*recto* and *verso*) from John 18. It is that famous scene where Pilate is interrogating Jesus and the subject of truth is raised. Jesus said that those who were of the truth would recognize His voice. Pilate responded, asking, "*What is truth?*" (John 18:38).

Not only did I spend time with the oldest New Testament fragment, I also took time with the second oldest fragment, P64 or the "Jesus fragment." P64 is actually three small fragments, all from Matthew 26, in which Jesus is anointed before His death. I hunted down this fragment in Oxford, which was located at Magdalen College (where C. S. Lewis studied and eventually taught until 1954) in the historic Old Library. P64 dates to the second century, yet it was not on display anywhere in the library. You can imagine my amazement when the helpful librarian handed me the fragment, which had been stored in something similar to a shoe box (but nicer) encased in glass. I said to her, "This fragment should be on display!" Think about it. These fragments are the earliest artifacts of Christianity. Indeed, it gives me great pleasure to say that the New Testament is well evidenced; the fragments are numerous; they are old; they exhibit linguistic, archeological, and cultural verisimilitude with the world of Jesus; and they overlap and corroborate with other extra-biblical sources. Therefore, we can say with confidence that the Bible we have today has been accurately preserved down through centuries, matching the original wording of the New Testament with 99 percent accuracy.

The wealth of manuscript material that is available for determining the wording of the original New Testament is striking. The New Testament is better attested to than any other ancient Greco-Roman literature, by far. We've already reviewed the fact that we have nearly six thousand Greek manuscripts of the New Testament. What about other languages? There are over ten thousand manuscripts in Latin and somewhere between five and ten thousand manuscripts in other ancient languages, like Coptic, Syriac, old-church Slavonic, Armenian, and more. This gives us a total of between twenty and twenty-five thousand New Testament manuscripts before the invention of moveable type by Johann Gutenberg in 1454–55, or as it is known now, the printing press. If I did not trust what the New Testament says about Jesus, then it would not be easy to be a Christian.

Textual criticism (that is, research of the text) has become one of the most important apologetic issues for the early twenty-first century. Textual criticism is the foundational science for investigating all literature prior to the printing press. The reason for this study is that all manuscripts prior to the printing press had differences among the many copies when compared to the original documents. This is true for the New Testament and it is true for all classical and Greek and Roman literature and virtually all other examples of ancient literature. We are required to do text criticism on all manuscripts before the invention of the printing press, precisely because no two manuscripts agree with each other due to the fact that they had to be copied by hand.

The Bible Is Experiential

The Scriptures promise that if you are committed to spend time with them, you will discover and attain the tools necessary to implement God's will for your life. It is a powerful statement to be able to confess, "I am in the center of God's will for my life!" Are you walking in God's perfect will for your life? Have you discovered your purpose? I discovered my purpose in life while studying the Scriptures, albeit very old fragments of the New Testament. On a cold, snowy, dark afternoon at Oxford, I was studying a third-century gospel of John fragment in the Griffith Papyrology Lab when God birthed the vision in my heart to launch our ministry, the Christian Thinkers Society. God was exposing me to the depths of His Word so I would be a channel. (See chapter 4.) Perhaps I can say it another way: had I not been studying biblical manuscripts, immersing myself in the Word of God, I am not convinced I would have ever discovered God's purpose for my life.

After seventy years of captivity, God raised up one man, Ezra, to lead His people back to Jerusalem and reclaim the land. The Old Testament book of Ezra is only ten chapters, but five times in those ten chapters it speaks of the good hand of God: *"the good hand of his God was on him"* (Ezra 7:9); *"the good hand of our God on us"* (Ezra 8:18). Ezra 7:6 states that Ezra was *"a scribe skilled in the Law of Moses."* Ezra was committed to the Word of God and God was committed to him. We are living in times of darkness and confusion, yet the Bible says, "*Your word is a lamp to my feet and a light to my path*" (Psalm 119:105).

Some of the blogs I read and the posts I see on social media remind me of Isaiah 5:20: "*Woe to those who call evil good and good evil, who put darkness for light and light for darkness, who put bitter for sweet and sweet for bitter!*" Have you noticed how confused you can become when you get away from God's Word? I have spent countless hours caring for families in churches and students at university and I can tell you that it is remarkable how the "fog of life" dissipates when there is a commitment to living in the light of God's Word. What new disciplines should you enact in your life to increase your commitment to God's Word?[127]

We can certainly review all of the reasons you should trust the Bible and its veracity, but if you have not committed yourself to experiencing it, it does you no good. Perhaps I can illustrate it this way. It is not enough to know the Bible intellectually if we do not encounter the Bible experientially. Yes, we should study the case for the Bible and know why we should trust its reliability, but that is not the end game. Here is a helpful exercise: take a look at your calendar for the previous month. How much time did you devote to God's Word? What passages have you mediated on? What Scriptures have you committed to memory?

My grandfather, John Wesley Johnston, discipled me for years. He is nearly ninety years old and continues teaching a Bible study every Sunday using the LifeWay curriculum. "JW," as we call Grandpa, reads his Bible through, from Genesis to Revelation, every eleven weeks. He reads five chapters per day and twenty on Sunday. For him, it has always been a discipline. It is astounding the wealth of wisdom one has when one reads the Bible through, four times per year.

My grandpa taught me some principles when I began seriously studying the Bible. He was of the opinion that you cannot learn a principle until you have applied it to your life. He taught me the "KD" principle: *know* (K) what the Word says, then *do* (D) it. JW also taught me the "MA" principle: I cannot know the Bible until I understand what it *means* (M), and I have not learned the Bible until I have *applied* (A) its meaning to my life. The famous Danish philosopher Søren Kierkegaard was fond of saying, "The

Bible is very easy to understand. But we Christians are a bunch of scheming swindlers. We pretend to be unable to understand it because we know very well that the minute we understand, we are obliged to act accordingly."

The Bible Brings Me Wisdom and Strength

Experiencing the Bible will not only lead us to discovering God's purpose, plan, and perfect will for our lives, but we will also gain wisdom. Have you considered the value of a good idea? Good ideas are extremely valuable. We all know the cost of making a bad decision, but prioritizing the Word of God will lead us to wisdom. Consider the value of making *one* good decision every day. Now envision making *five* good decisions every day. The value of those good decisions will multiply exponentially in your family, marriage, and employment. James 1:25 is a promise: *"But one who looks intently at the perfect law, the law of liberty, and abides by it, not having become a forgetful hearer but an effectual doer, this man will be blessed in what he does"* (NASB).

Our desire should be to be the people of Psalm 1:2–3:

> *...but his delight is in the law of the* Lord, *and on his law he meditates day and night. He is like a tree planted by streams of water that yields its fruit in its season, and its leaf does not wither. In all that he does, he prospers.*

If you read the Bible fifteen minutes per day, you can read the Bible through from Genesis to Revelation in one year. Do you have fifteen minutes a day you can dedicate to almighty God? Take a moment and prayerfully examine your priorities. Then I encourage you to get on your knees, open your calendar/schedule book, and lay them before God and pray something like, "God, I am going to rearrange my priorities to experience You in Your Word. You are going to have first position in my life, even if that means rearranging my schedule and priorities."

> *Your words were found, and I ate them, and your words became to me a joy and the delight of my heart.* (Jeremiah 15:16)

If you are in the Word of God, you will successfully resist temptation and avoid compromise in your life. In Matthew 4, Jesus repeatedly said, "*It is written,*" and quoted Deuteronomy to resist the devil. (See verses 4, 7, 10.)

If you are experiencing God in His Word, you will have strength and wisdom, but make no mistake, you also will have stability. All the effective Christian leaders I know are men and women who are deeply committed to spending time daily with God in His Word. Their lives are marked by stability. I have read biographies of men who read all the epistles in their Greek New Testament, twice every night before going to bed. Joshua Barnes, a professor at Cambridge in the 1700s, carried a little pocket Bible and said he read it through one hundred twenty times by the time of his death. Robert Cotton, a Puritan, read through the entire Bible twelve times per year.

The Story of the Bible

The Bible is a love story. Really, it is the greatest break-up-and-get-back-together-story the world has ever known. Most of my students are visual learners and so I use well-known movie plots to describe the meta-narrative of the Bible. Not surprisingly, most of my female students can share most if not all of the plot details in Nicholas Sparks's *The Notebook*. Using similar plot points I guide my students by the hand on a journey of the fall-in-love (God's love for us), break-up (the fall), and get-back-together (Jesus and redemption) story of the Bible. The message of the Bible is that even though we are not what we should be, God loves us and has a purpose for our lives. He knows us by name. He desires an eternal relationship with us. He seeks us out.

Have you personally experienced the Bible's message? It is one thing to perhaps know some of the aspects of the Bible's story, but it is an altogether different reality to have experienced the message of the Bible. Have you fallen for the love story of the Bible? God's Word speaks to the ultimate questions of life: Who am I? Why I am here? What is the purpose and meaning of my life?

While living in Oxford, I was invited to Corpus Christi College at Cambridge, through my friend, Dr. Pete Williams, warden of Tyndale House. A medieval professor, Dr. Chris de Hamel hosted us in the historic Parker Library. When we arrived Professor de Hamel had a stack of volumes sitting on a table, which he claimed were valued at more than ten million pounds sterling. (He said we were in august company, as Pope Benedict had been the previous guest of the library.) This was a profound experience for me as a doctoral student. I carefully looked at autographs (originals) of Erasmus (1466–1536), John Calvin (1509–1564), Martin Luther (1483–1546), King Alfred (849–899) and a very rare letter from Anne Boleyn (1501–1536) to William Tyndale (1494–1536).

Indeed, Anne Boleyn has been affectionately called the "Martin Luther of England," because she was a leading figure in the development of Protestantism in England. "Anne of a Thousand Days," as she is known due to her short reign (from age 26 to 29, 1533–1536), was executed only five months before Tyndale was executed. Boleyn was a champion of using her influence to ensure an English Bible was created and disseminated throughout England. In 1534, Anne was presented with a copy of William Tyndale's New Testament, complete with her coat of arms marked on the title page. This offers us a glimpse of their boldness. Tyndale's New Testament was a banned book. Possessing it was punishable by death. As much as the authorities tried to stop him, Tyndale's influence could not be suppressed. The words that Tyndale translated are more well know today than those of Shakespeare, and certainly used with more frequency, though most people do not recognize they are quoting a Tyndalism: "*Let there be light*" (Genesis 1:3); "*a man after his own heart*" (1 Samuel 13:14); "*the salt of the earth*" (Matthew 5:13); "*the truth will set you free*" (John 8:32); "*fight the good fight*" (1 Timothy 6:12). Tyndale gave God an English voice. The story of the Bible is Jesus; He is the silver lining of every page. Tyndale said, "The Scripture is a light, and shows us the true way both what to do and what to hope for...in Christ Jesus our Lord."[128]

If it were possible to time travel, my preference would be to go to Europe in the early sixteenth century. What an era! Tyndale, Luther, Erasmus, and other giants of the faith, critically thinking through the issues of the day. Their voices now ripple through history. Similar to Luther in Germany,

Tyndale lived with a bounty on his head in England and the Continent. Tyndale dared to defy the crown and the Roman Catholic Church by translating and disseminate the Bible into English. Tyndale's life work was to make the Bible accessible for everyone. He paid for it, dearly. Unlike Luther, Tyndale was martyred at the age of forty-two. This gifted man, able to speak eight languages, each as if it was his native tongue, was reduced to ash in a morning, burned at the stake.

In his magisterial biography, David Danielle notes that Tyndale's charge was "heresy, with not agreeing with the Holy Roman Emperor—in a nutshell, being a Lutheran."[129] Tyndale was betrayed by a friend in 1535 and was executed on October 6, 1536. He spent his final sixteen months (five hundred days) wasting away in a dungeon at Vilvoorde Castle, six miles north of Brussels. His captors confiscated his books and belongings and sold them off, which means that Tyndale essentially self-financed his own prison term.[130] Can you imagine? His crime was translating the Bible. Fourteen years after Tyndale's execution, Roger Asham, mentor and teacher to a young princess named Elizabeth (daughter of Anne Boleyn), paid his respects at Vilvoorde, and later said, "At the town's end is a notable solemn place of execution, where worthy William Tyndale was unworthily put to death."[131] Eight years after Asham's visit, (*c.* 1558), Elizabeth became Queen of England and reigned for forty-four years. Tyndale's influence on Elizabeth heralded a new dawn of Bible translation, publication, and dissemination through all of England.

The English Bible we have today stands squarely on the shoulders of Tyndale's Bible. Eighty-three percent of the King James Version is Tyndale's translation work. Prior to the printing of Tyndale's New Testament (*c.* 1525), the only English Bible that was scarcely available was Wycliffe's Bible, which was handwritten in "Chaucerian" Medieval English and translated from the Latin Vulgate. A common person could not afford this Bible, the price around forty pounds sterling, the equivalent of several years' wages. It took ten months to produce a single copy. The lucky ones were able to afford to purchase a single page. What made Tyndale's Bible so helpful was the fact that not only were the words understandable, but it also was affordable, and, due to its small size, could be transported clandestinely.

In any case, Tyndale, being the scholar that he was, was the first to translate the New Testament into English (*c.* 1526, first edition) from the original Greek, using the newly printed Greek edition produced by Erasmus (*c.* 1516). It is debated whether three thousand or six thousand copies of Tyndale's first edition New Testament were printed. Tyndale's printed New Testament was missional and creative. The end game was not simply a printed book, but one that could easily trade hands and be passed along. Tyndale's New Testament was printed in a stealth-like, pocket-sized format so it could be smuggled into and throughout England. Similar to North Korea today, where owning a Bible is a capital offense, possessing Tyndale's New Testament was grounds for execution. (See chapter 14, when in 1407, Archbishop Thomas Arundel passed the Constitutions of Oxford, effectively outlawing the reading, translating, or possession of an English Bible.) The Bishop of London, Cuthbert Tunstall (1474–1559) and other authorities did their best to confiscate Tyndale's New Testament. They were effective. Only three copies of Tyndale's first edition survive today. In 1994, the British Library purchased a single copy of Tyndale's 1526 New Testament for one million pounds from Bristol Baptist College. It was dubbed "the most important printed book in the English language."[132] The British Library adds that "it had cost just 20 guineas in the first half of the 18th century when Edward Harley, Lord of Oxford, added the book to his already extensive library."[133] If you are ever in London, be certain to pay a visit to the British Library and gaze upon this treasure.

I hope that one of the outcomes from this section is that you will be convinced that the Bible was precious in the days of Luther and Tyndale, and that it should be precious today, as well. As I finished my time at the Parker Library in Cambridge I was awestruck by what a miracle it is that we have a Bible to read at all. I also left challenged, because I realized that 95 percent of people in the pews do not know these courageous and daring stories of how the Bible came to be in the first place. These stories capture our hearts, stretch our imagination, and strengthen our faith. Indeed, they must be shared. The Bible has been suppressed, banned, burned, outlawed, and yet it remains.[134] Our older Christian brothers and sisters did not sacrifice their lives so that we could have a Bible in our own language and never read it—a Bible-*ish* Christianity. Honor the Bible, experience the Bible, invest your life in the Bible, because, in the words of Simon Peter, "*Lord, to whom shall we go? You have the words of eternal life*" (John 6:68).

Before you turn the page, my prayer is that you will take a moment for prayer and reflection on what you have learned in chapters 14 and 15. To aid you in your meditation, I encourage you to prayerfully review the words of John Burton, a Sunday school teacher who, in 1803, wrote the hymn "Holy Book, Book Divine":

Holy Bible, Book Divine,

Precious treasure, thou art mine;
Mine to tell me whence I came;
Mine to teach me what I am.

Mine to chide me when I rove,
Mine to shew a Savior's love;
Mine thou art to guide and guard;
Mine to punish or reward.

Mine to comfort in distress,
Suffering in this wilderness;
Mine to show by living faith,
We can triumph over death.

Mine to tell of joys to come,
And the rebel sinner's doom;
O thou holy book divine,
Precious treasure thou art mine.[135]

16

ENGAGEMENT PRINCIPLE #4: BE CURIOUS

This principle of engagement presupposes the fact that most people love to talk about themselves. It never ceases to amaze me what someone will tell you if they know you are listening. Ask questions, ask questions, and ask more questions. Be willing to make the person you are talking with the expert. Over and over again, I have found that individuals respond so much more to an inquisitive conversation than to an assertion. Questions make the conversation a two-way process. No one wants to be dictated to. Questions are conversational and can be flattering.

A byproduct of being curious is that our questions will grow very quickly, which will stimulate the conversation to continue. It does not take long or require much effort to be curious; have you noticed? Being curious can also help other individuals doubt their doubts. Audiences always get a perplexed look when I say that we must doubt our doubts. I actually do not think there is enough doubt, because people are so accepting of their doubts. Doubting should apply to all belief systems. Doubting should apply to everything. As people, we vacillate and we are not all that stable. This is a human characteristic. Why do we take our doubts so seriously? We need to doubt the doubts. Being curious or asking the right questions will help others doubt the reasons why they doubt. We live in a world that is a lot like first-century Rome, a world that is growing increasingly secular. We need to do a better job disseminating good reasons for the Christian faith.

The right question is the onramp to a better conclusion. Being curious, therefore, can lead to a turning point. The problem is that most people do not understand each other all that well. Atheists, by and large, do not understand religious people. Christians do not understand atheists all that well, either. Asking questions is the best way to understand your audience. Start sharing your faith by asking questions. Questions bring a response and encourage conversation. Questions linger on after the conversation is over.

There are so many false ideas about Jesus, the Bible, and the modern church. People do not know much, if anything, about the biblical-historical Jesus. We need to correct mistaken notions and uncritical thinking, as it relates to our faith. We need to ask questions now more than ever and engage in sincere dialogue with people with whom we disagree. Surveying the Gospels, one will notice that Jesus used curiosity as a teaching method and approach to evangelism. I encourage you to study every question Jesus asked, as recorded in the Gospels. (Hint: there are well over one hundred questions.) You will notice that Jesus' questions left an impression. Jesus was all-knowing and still He was curious. Let us follow His example for effective engagement.

PART 6

BECOMING JOB: WHY SUFFERING, ME-CENTRIC CHRISTIANITY, AND A CONCIERGE-GOD DON'T MIX

17

PREVENT FAITH: WHY I NEED A BEND-BUT-DON'T-BREAK BELIEF

There are people in life who leave lasting impressions. The sermons they preach by the way they live their lives are far more powerful than sermons preached with words.

July 30 was a Sunday I will never forget. Rejoicing after a weekend of services, my phone rang. It was my friend Marty and I was not prepared for what he would share with me in the moments that followed.

The context is always important when sharing a story. Marty, and his wife Karen, attended our church reluctantly at first. There were a lot of people, there were TV cameras, and colored lights, but they were attracted to the teaching. Slowly we came to know one another. We traveled together on our Bible Land tours throughout Greece, Turkey, and Israel. I developed a close bond with this family. Marty and Karen have two talented children. Their son, Anthony, an incredible entrepreneur, who cofounded a famous shoe and apparel company, was in his early thirties. While visiting his parents, Anthony attended our church and I was struck by what he said after the service: "I like how you all do church."

Anthony had a home in Scottsdale, Arizona, and invited us to share Thanksgiving there together. It was all good. Now, back to that phone call.

Ten days after meeting Anthony, my phone rang. "Jeremiah, this is Marty. Anthony died; he is with Jesus." Anthony had been feeling unwell after a golf tournament that was held in his honor. He went home and passed away in his sleep at the age of thirty-six. I was shocked by Marty's call. We presided at the funeral. Notably, what I recall most about the funeral service was hearing people pray aloud to trust Christ as their Savior.

Marty and Karen, grieving as any parent would, kept repeating, "We're going to trust God." Indeed, it is a parent's worst nightmare to outlive their children, and Marty and Karen were living that nightmare. Unfortunately, their suffering did not end there. Bereaved, Marty said that he was beginning to notice bouts of blurred vision. He went to a specialist only to learn that he had a brain tumor.

Can you imagine losing your child and then being diagnosed with a brain tumor? I did my best to minister to Marty and Karen, but more than anything else, I wanted to be present. When people are hurting, you do not have to say anything. In fact, most of the time, it is best to say nothing at all. Audrey and I spent time with Marty and Karen in two different hospitals, in two different states, as they sought treatment for his tumor. I will never forget visiting Marty post-surgery. He had a fever, he was in obvious pain, but he kept saying, "I'm going to trust God."

The good news is that God healed Marty's brain tumor, but the sting of losing his son remains and will never leave. There were many moments of grieving with Marty and Karen, yet in the midst of their suffering, not once do I remember them complaining. They trusted God through the loss of a son and during a difficult illness. Marty and Karen are not ordained, nor do they have advanced degrees in theology, yet they evidenced a trust in God that calls to mind the words of Jesus to the centurion: "*I tell you, not even in Israel have I found such faith*" (Luke 7:9).

Have you ever hurt so deeply that, like Marty and Karen, you felt like death? Have you experienced chronic depression so devastating that you actually wished to die? Perhaps you have experienced a loss that has caused you to abandon hope. Do you know that there is a powerful passage in the Bible in which one of the strongest followers of Jesus also wished to die?

The Job of the New Testament: Paul

In 2 Corinthians 1, the apostle Paul was writing to the church he had founded at Corinth in AD 50. Paul was hurting so deeply that only God could comfort him. We learn of Paul's sufferings as we open 2 Corinthians. Even though this letter is known as "Second" Corinthians, it is most likely the fourth letter he sent to the Corinthian church family. Paul preached for eighteen months in the city during his second missionary journey. (See Acts 18.) He knew the Corinthians well. They were safe. He could be brutally honest with them. It is helpful to note that of all the letters Paul wrote to the churches he founded, none are longer than 1 and 2 Corinthians.

I Can and Should Be Honest about the Reality of My Suffering and Pain

Paul's revealing letter is emblematic of the fact that Christians should never be afraid to be transparent about the reality of their suffering and pain. Where did we get this notion that sharing honestly about our pain and suffering is somehow un-Christian? You do not lack faith if you share your pain. In 2 Corinthians 1:8, Paul was extremely honest about all of his problems, pain, suffering and the evil he experienced in his life and ministry. Did you know the book of 2 Corinthians has been called the "Job of the New Testament"? Paul, like Job, faced so many problems that his critics and opponents claimed he was not actually an apostle, because it was apparent that God had abandoned him. Paul responded by arguing that his suffering was, in fact, the very mark of his apostleship. (See 2 Corinthians 3:1–18.) Paul declared, *"We do not lose heart"* (2 Corinthians 4:1), even though his reality was one of brokenness and suffering, *"afflicted in every way, but not crushed"* (verse 8).

Paul confessed, *"For we do not want you to be unaware, brethren, of our affliction which came to us in Asia, that we were burdened excessively, beyond our strength, so that we* ***despaired*** *even of life"* (2 Corinthians 1:8 NASB). I encourage you to underline the word *"despaired"* in your Bible, from the Greek *exaporeomai*. This word gives us a measurement of the pain in Paul's life. He had renounced all hope. He felt there was no escape from his suffering; he *"despaired even of life."* Have you ever been there? Some translations and paraphrases render it suffering *"beyond our ability to endure"* (NIV, NLT). Paul suffered to the extent that it not only affected him physically but it also afflicted him spiritually. He was unable to comprehend the suffering.

Have you noticed that most of the time our suffering does not make sense? Suffering is so often unexplainable. Paul continued, *"indeed, we had the* ***sentence of death*** *within ourselves"* (verse 9 NASB). Underline *"sentence of death"* in verse nine. *"Sentence"* is the Greek word *apokrima*, the word's only occurrence in the New Testament. This gives us a greater appreciation for Paul's transparency. In classical Greek, this word refers to an official verdict as a pronouncement. Notice where he had received this verdict *"within ourselves."* Paul was in such pain that he felt, within himself, that he was on death row. We can imagine Paul thought, *I am so overwhelmed; I am so stressed; I am so anxious; I think I am going to die!* The tense is important because it is the Greek perfect tense, which means he felt he was under a permanent sentence of suffering. He did not think his suffering would end.

This is a significant point for us as we attempt to live a vibrant faith while also enduring intense suffering. Paul did not deny his feelings. Paul did not gloss over how he was really doing. Therefore, if you are having a tough day or a difficult time, it is okay for you to talk about it. Doing so brings healing. It is healthy to discuss your struggles. Paul certainly did.

Later in the epistle, we notice Paul experienced *"afflictions, hardships, calamities"* (2 Corinthians 6:4); *"beatings, imprisonments, riots, sleepless nights, hunger"* (verse 5); *"honor and dishonor...slander and praise"* (verse 8); *"unknown, and yet well known...dying, and behold, we live...punished, and yet not killed"* (verse 9); *"sorrowful, yet always rejoicing...poor, yet making many rich...having nothing, yet possessing everything"* (verse 10).

If you are struggling, share that fact with your pastor, your spouse, or a trusted friend. Do not bottle it up. Through this story we learn that God does not want us to deny our emotions. Later in 2 Corinthians, Paul wrote, *"For indeed, when we came to Macedonia, our bodies had no rest, but we were troubled on every side. Outside were conflicts, inside were fears"* (2 Corinthians 7:5 NKJV). Discussing your problems does not equate to a lack of faith. This is my frustration with some Christian media personalities. They demand we only speak positively. They demand we always claim victory. They seem to insist that we ignore the reality of our suffering and simply "declare" otherwise. The undertone is that if you are honest about your pain, you must not have enough faith. This is harmful and unhealthy. Defining the reality of your situation leads to healing.

Never forget that Paul began his letter saying, *"we do not want you to be unaware, brethren, of our affliction"* (2 Corinthians 1:8 NASB). You may have been raised in a family in which struggles were never discussed. There are some families who suffer, experience setbacks, and yet they refuse to talk about it. Fights occur, the silent treatment (sometimes lasting days) ensues. But the conflict is never discussed. Emotions become entangled. This is the worst-case scenario. Or, in many cases of suicide, due to a sense of shame, people left behind act as if the event never happened. Not discussing your troubles will lead to more heartache.

Paul Recalled the Past but He Did Not Live There

I am convinced that we learn from the past but we should not live there. Many people live in their past. Indeed, they seem unable to escape it. Though Paul is eager and transparent in recalling his suffering, he does not live there. Notice where Paul's focus is: "*indeed, we had the sentence of death within ourselves so that we would not trust in ourselves, but in God who raises the dead; who delivered us from so great a peril of death, and will deliver us, He on whom we have set our hope. And* ***He will yet deliver us***" (2 Corinthians 1:9–10 NASB). I find it interesting that as Paul opens this letter, he is aware of his challenges but his focus is on God, "*the Father of mercies and God of all comfort*" (verse 3 NASB). Paul had learned the lesson that every overcomer eventually understands: learn from the past but don't live there. Paul had his share of troubles and significant challenges, but he had been comforted by God, and as a result, he was able to comfort the troubled Corinthian church family.

While Paul's trials brought him physical and emotional pain, perplexity, and sorrow, he was strengthened by the encouragement of God. Therefore, Paul was able to thank God for his trials, rejoice in them, and use the lessons he learned to encourage others. Our focus must remain on God when we struggle, suffer, and experience pain. For Paul and his companions, their trials taught them to "*not trust in ourselves, but in God who raises the dead*" (2 Corinthians 1:9 NASB).

Notice, in 2 Corinthians 1:3, Paul's confident trust and assurance is whole-heartedly placed in the "*God of all comfort*." Our best translation of the English word "*comfort*," translated from the Greek word *paráklēsisis,* is encouragement! We serve a God who is encouraging in spite of life's greatest difficulties. Indeed, He is the God of all encouragement. Paul knew the strength of almighty God. In another passage, Paul wrote of God's strengths, which worked mightily through him. (See Colossians 1:29.) The comfort only God provides is the comfort that brings courage and enables a person to cope with all that life brings, because of the One who is always at his or her side!

In Ralph Martin's commentary of 2 Corinthians, he renders 2 Corinthians 1:3–7:

> Blessed (be) the God and Father of our Lord Jesus Christ, the Father of mercies and the God of all encouragement. He encourages us in all our trial, so that we can encourage those who are in any trial by the (same) encouragement with which we ourselves

> are encouraged by God. For just as Christ's sufferings overflow to us, so also does the encouragement that we receive through Christ overflow. If we are facing trials, it is for your encouragement and salvation. If we are encouraged, it is for your encouragement which (God) produces as you remain steadfast under the same sufferings that we suffer. And our hope for you is firmly grounded, because we know that, as you share the sufferings, so too (you share) in the encouragement.[136]

In five verses (2 Corinthians 1:3–7) Paul makes use of the word *"comfort"* (encouragement) ten times! No wonder Paul could speak often about his privilege and joy in sharing in the sufferings of Christ. (See, for example, Romans 8:17; Philippians 3:10; Colossians 1:24.) As did the apostle Peter. (See, for example, 1 Peter 4:13; 5:1.) Followers of Jesus are called to endure suffering as Christ suffered in order to experience an even closer union with Him. Christians are called to bear reproach, rejection, hostility, denial, and even hatred. Why? Because we serve a God who is all-encouraging.

I grew up in the Midwest, in a region known as "tornado alley." We had tornado drills, sirens on the first Wednesday of every month, everyone knew where the shelters were located, and tornado watches and warnings were part of the fabric of spring and summer life. Despite all this preparation, most tornado casualties were often the result of unpreparedness. The same is true for Christians. The Bible has many storm warnings about life and hardship. We cannot pick and choose the Bible verses we like and ignore the ones that are more challenging. Just because we have become followers of Jesus does not mean we live free from the storms of life. Sadly, some people reveal their Christian immaturity when they suffer. Many Christians in the West have embraced a theology that rests on the fallacy that nothing bad should happen to you after you become a Christian. Then, when trials, tests, and tragedies come—and make no mistake, they will come—they find that their faith is undermined, a faith that was based only on experiencing happiness in this life.

Authentic Christian faith is never surprised by adversity and problems. In *If God Is Good,* author Randy Alcorn wrote, "The faith that can't be shaken is the faith that has been shaken."[137] God is faithful, and our faith is refined when we suffer, because we learn by experience that God is good and trustworthy: "*Behold, I have refined you, but not as silver; I have tried you in the furnace of affliction*" (Isaiah 48:10; see also Job 23:10; Romans 2:7; 1 Peter 1:7).

Let's self-correct our mistaken theology. The ultimate purpose of life is not our happiness but rather the knowledge of God derived through a relationship with Jesus Christ. Who is this God who has made innumerable promises to us in His Word? Shouldn't we get to know Him? Do you believe in a concierge God? One reason the problem of evil has so much traction is that many Western Christians assume that if God exists, then His purpose for my life is my personal comfort and happiness—because it's all about me. We become perplexed during times of suffering if we have a mind-set that being a Christian means we will never suffer! A biblical worldview, however, explains that God is not a cosmic concierge service and the purpose of human life is not personal happiness. Our purpose is to know God, make Him known, glorify Him, and proclaim His plan of salvation to the world. God created you with a purpose. We come to know God better in our trials. When the New Testament addresses the problems of evil, suffering, and tragedy, the emphasis is not on the cause of the suffering, nor is it on a miraculous escape from the suffering; instead, the New Testament affirms the presence of Jesus in times of crisis, what is to be learned, who we are to become, and how we should respond. The Westminster Shorter Catechism asks the question "What is the chief end of man?" and provides the answer: "To glorify God and to enjoy Him forever."

In chapter 3 I touched on the fact that my wife and I have visited some of the most lethal places on earth in which to be recognized as a Christian. Our interactions with Chinese Christians, who are courageous enough to survive, forgive, love, and most of all, believe amidst atheistic aggression, has been life changing. In some of the countries where Christians experience the most intense persecution, the church is expanding exponentially. What was true in the book of Acts is true today. There is a symbiotic relationship between growth rates of Christianity and suffering in the world. The more the church is persecuted, the more it is made uncomfortable and the more its mission expands! As a modern example consider there are now more Christians than communists in China. Recent surveys calculate the number of mainland Christians worshiping independently of state churches to be as many as one hundred million people. Nearly one in ten Chinese people are Christians. That means there are more Chinese Christians in the world than American Christians!

Romans 5:20 has been a guidepost for my life, especially when I face *"trials of various kinds"* (James 1:2). Romans 5:20 promises *"where sin increased, grace abounded all the more."* In Greek, this passage promises a "super-abounding" (*huperperisseúō*) or "lavish" grace. You can experience God's lavish grace, too. God supplies super-abounding grace for us, all of us, to withstand the suffering we experience in our lives.

When Christians suffer, we have a confident expectation: God is in total control. In October 1871, the Great Chicago Fire reduced significant portions of the city to ashes. D. L. Moody was preaching that Sunday evening when the inferno began to spread and did not know if his children had survived until twenty-four hours later. Emma Moody later recalled that her mother's hair began turning gray that night, overcome with worry and anxiety at the thought of the inferno taking her children. Little did Mrs. Moody know that her dear friends the Spaffords had saved her children from the fire and taken them to their home in Buena Park. This was the same Spafford family who only a few years later would suffer the loss of their four little girls in the sinking of the *Ville du Havre* in the mid-Atlantic. Moody biographer Kevin Belmonte tells the rest of the story:

> ...sometimes history converges in unforgettable ways. The terrible sea disaster became the inspiration for Horatio Spafford to share his enduring faith by writing, "It Is Well with my Soul," the now classic hymn. It staggers the imagination to think that the Spaffords were able to help save the Moody children but would later suffer the loss of their own four daughters.[138]

The apostle Paul had a bend-but-don't-break faith. I love football and if you do not, I hope you will forgive the analogy. When a team is leading by several touchdowns late in the game, a coach will often call for a "prevent" defense. This defense spreads out the defensive players and places a number of them deep downfield to "prevent" the other team from scoring touchdowns and reducing the lead. This bend-but-don't-break defense is not concerned with giving up yards, just touchdowns. As it relates to suffering, we need to be like Paul and put it all on the field; we need an emboldened faith that can bend but will not break. The question of evil, suffering, and pain cannot be answered in one hundred forty characters or less—sorry Twitter. Unfortunately, we live in a society that prefers sound bites over substance. A significant question deserves a substantial answer. Therefore, we'll return to 2 Corinthians 1 in the next chapter as we answer the question about "the problem of love."

18

THE PROBLEM OF LOVE

No one can deny that Steve Jobs was one of the most iconic people of our time. His innovations have shaped and connected the world—no wonder he appeared on the cover of *Time* magazine eight times between 1982 and 2011. Jobs had an unanswered question, which, tragically, caused him to walk away from his Christian faith. It happened at a young age. Jobs's official biography was published less than three weeks after his death in October 2011, based on forty interviews conducted in the two years preceding his unfortunate passing at the age of fifty-six. Biographer Walter Isaacson wrote these chilling words about Jobs's loss of faith at the age of thirteen due to an unanswered question:

> In July 1968 *Life* magazine published a shocking cover showing a pair of starving children in Biafra. Jobs took it to Sunday school

> and confronted the church's pastor. "If I raise my finger, will God know which one I'm going to raise even before I do it?" The pastor answered, "Yes, God knows everything." Jobs then pulled out the *Life* cover and asked, "Well, does God know about this and what's going to happen to those children?" "Steve, I know you don't understand, but yes, God knows about that." Jobs announced that he didn't want to have anything to do with worshipping such a God, and he never went back to church.[139]

Suffering in the world, and a God that allows it, caused thirteen-year-old Steve Jobs to rethink and turn away from his faith. It might surprise you to learn that out of the thousands of questions we have received at CTS, I have never been asked a question relating to God, the Bible, or the difficulties of life that was not first asked somewhere in the Bible. The familiar passage in Job 14:1 reminds us all that *"man who is born of a woman is few of days and full of trouble,"* and perhaps the greatest trouble most struggle with is that of tragedy and suffering. Indeed, the number one reason people walk away from faith is the personal experience of unexpected tragedy.

The Rain Falls on the Just and the Unjust

In 2015 our Christian Thinkers Society team filmed interviews at the National American Atheism Convention in Memphis, Tennessee. We asked many of the atheists the "why" question: Why did you become an atheist? Several answers were offered. One atheist, a former Catholic, became an atheist in his Old Testament class at divinity school. Another atheist, a former Southern Baptist, said that the lack of critical thinking skills drove him to question everything about his faith.

Two reasons enforcing their entrenched atheism were offered in nearly every interview: suffering in the world and the lack of critical thinking. These were the main arguments undergirding their atheism. Their answers were revealing. "The world is not as it ought to be," said most of the atheists we filmed. Think about it carefully; that answer infers a standard of objective, worldwide virtue and goodness. According to the atheist, when we are dead, there is nothing more—no afterlife, no post-mortem existence. Life is a cosmic accident that is of no intrinsic value. However, if there is no God and no afterlife, and the material world (what we can experience with our five senses) is all that exists, why would we expect anything good in our lives now?

Jesus said, *"For* [God] *makes his sun rise on the evil and on the good, and sends rain on the just and on the unjust"* (Matthew 5:45). Many people find it hard to reconcile the simultaneous existence of both evil and a caring God. Does God really love me if He allows me to experience tragedy? An atheist friend once asked, "If God exists, why doesn't He show up and visit a children's hospital?"

Do you know what my answer is? God does "show up," through His church.

While you are answering the problem of evil, you must answer the problem of love, too. Why are there so many wonderful things in the world? Why do we love? The message of Christianity explains why there is grace, beauty, love, and *"on earth peace, good will toward men"* (Luke 2:14 KJV). The message of the cross inspires many people, who—in the face of great adversity—sacrifice, care, love, and go to extreme measures for noble purposes. Christianity makes sense of why people try to behave well and do the right thing. From the earliest days, the Christian movement has taught and believed *"for God so loved the world"* (John 3:16)—that is, all of His creation, everyone created in His image. Did you know that Islam teaches that Allah does not love non-Muslims? (See Qur'an 30:45; 3:32; 22:38.) At one time, C. S. Lewis had this idea, too:

> My argument against God was that the universe seemed so cruel and unjust. But how had I got this idea of just and unjust? A man does not call a line crooked unless he has some idea of a straight line. What was I comparing this universe with when I called it unjust? If the whole show was bad and senseless from A to Z, so to speak, why did I, who was supposed to be part of the show, find myself in such violent reaction against it?...Thus in the very act of trying to prove that God did not exist—in

> other words, that the whole of reality was senseless—I found I was forced to assume that one part of reality—namely my idea of justice—was full of sense. Consequently atheism turns out to be too simple. If the whole universe has no meaning, we should never have found out that it has no meaning: just as, if there were no light in the universe and therefore no creatures with eyes, we should never know it was dark. Dark would be without meaning.[140]

It Takes the Fire to Bring Out the Music

Charles Spurgeon (1834–1892) is known as the "prince of preachers," but the London papers once called him "a ranting charlatan." On October 19, 1856, at the age of twenty-two, Spurgeon stood to preach at the Surrey Gardens Music Hall to a capacity crowd of more than ten thousand people. According to Spurgeon biographer Arnold Dallimore, this was very likely, in its day, the largest indoor audience to ever assemble to hear the gospel. The service began with music and everything seemed normal. However, when Spurgeon began to lead the massive congregation in prayer, someone in the balcony screamed, "Fire!" Pandemonium ensued. Masses of humanity charged the exits of the building. Unable to sustain the immense weight, a stair railing fell and seven people were crushed to death and another twenty-eight people were injured. Spurgeon was so overcome with grief that he "fell to the floor, almost unconscious." In view of this tragedy, he seriously contemplated giving up. This reminds me of the principle that I learned early in my ministry: never make a decision when you are discouraged or fatigued. For a week and a half, Spurgeon flirted with ending his ministry, but one day, on a stroll in a garden, God radiated His presence into Spurgeon's soul with the words of Philippians 2:9–11: "*Therefore God has highly exalted him and bestowed on him the name that is above every name, so that at the name of Jesus every knee should bow, in heaven and on earth and under the earth, and every tongue confess that Jesus Christ is Lord, to the glory of God the Father.*" The name of Jesus can transcend suffering and loss.

Spurgeon mounted the pulpit the following Sunday and kept going. In his 1894 biography, *The Prince of Preachers*, James Douglas wrote:

> Charles Haddon Spurgeon was in no respect ordinary. He was great as a man; great as a theologian; great as a preacher; great in private with God; and great in public with his fellow men. He was well versed in three things, which, according to Luther, make a minister: temptation, meditation and prayer. The school of suffering was one in which he was deeply taught.[141]

In the ten years from 1875–1885, Spurgeon's ministry reached its apex, though he so rarely was able to enjoy the fruits of his ministry, suffering with frequent and chronic depression. In this golden era of Spurgeon's preaching, his beloved wife, Susannah, was so unwell that she was considered to be an invalid, unable to minister to her husband in his constant battles in the darkness of depression. Spurgeon, referencing Bunyan's *The Pilgrim's Progress*, said he was a frequent prisoner "in the dungeons underneath the Castle of Despair."

On one particularly difficult evening, Spurgeon visited his wife's room. As he sat gazing into the crackling fire, he listened to the symphony of sounds echoing in the vacuous room. As a fire burns, it consumes and decomposes the wood into several forms of gas (smoke), char, and ash, which for Spurgeon, produced a swift musical tone. Pulling himself up by his bootstraps, Spurgeon whispered to his wife, "Susannah, it takes the fire to bring out the music."[142]

Spurgeon's success in the nineteenth century was unrivaled, his influence unmatched. Perched in his study, surrounded by his massive library consisting of twelve thousand volumes, he produced more than one hundred forty literary works, as well as weekly sermons that were published and distributed far beyond the Metropolitan Tabernacle, and it was estimated that he wrote five hundred letters per week. He was a man of his time. He would not allow his suffering to paralyze him. Spurgeon's focus, like that of Paul in 2 Corinthians 1, was not on his suffering but on the God of all encouragement, who meets us in our suffering.

Our Response to Suffering Determines Our Destiny

The cone snail can grow to only a few inches in length, but its venom is deadly enough to kill more than twenty adult humans. One of the symptoms of a cone snail's sting is paralysis. Human suffering can start small, like the cone snail, but it also can lead to paralysis. Recently our two-year-old son had a major kidney operation that required a multiple-night stay in the hospital. My wife and I felt numb as we watched our son, unable to do anything to allay his pain. We felt paralyzed. It was difficult to talk. Watching a child suffer can make it difficult for some to believe in God. Experiencing our two-year-old son suffer through the recovery process clouded our intellectual answers for why this was happening.

When you experience suffering, you cannot allow it to cause emotional or spiritual paralysis. You must focus on God. In chapter 17 we began studying a few verses in 2 Corinthians 1, and we noted that Paul revisited his past sufferings but he did not live there. (See verses 8–9.) Paul's focus was on our all-encouraging God, who raises the dead; who, in fact, has already delivered us; and who, despite delivering us, will ultimately deliver us. (See verses 9–10.)

Have you noticed that when we suffer, sometimes we can be tempted to rely on our own strength more than God's strength? It is as if we say, "You know what, God? You can take some time off; I've got this." And then we don't...have it. We grow in maturity as Christians when we learn to put our faith in God alone and not in our abilities to negotiate a way out of the pain. Paul said that we are to live daily in the light of sacrifice (see Romans 12:1–2), but have you noticed how often we want to crawl away from the altar of being a living sacrifice?

The syntax in 2 Corinthians 1:9 is helpful *"so that we would not trust in ourselves* [a negative], *but in God* [a positive] *who raises the dead"* (NASB). Paul's suffering took him to the brink—a brink at which we all must arrive—and God stripped him down and took away every trace of confidence he might have had in himself. Paul was utterly dependent on God. God makes it possible to absorb and transcend suffering. Only through God can we improve and advance in the Refiner's fire of pain. Paul expressed his theology in a phrase: "*...not trust in ourselves, but in God who raises the dead.*" Paul described God in two ways in 2 Corinthians 1: first, as a God who comforts or encourages (see verse 4), and second, as a God who raises the dead (see verse 9). Paul needed nothing more. God will comfort me; He will see me through the dark night, and out of this misery. He will work a miracle.

In 2 Timothy 4:16–17, Paul revisited his experience of standing alone, yet not totally alone: "*At my first defense no one came to stand by me, but all deserted me....But the Lord stood by me and strengthened me....I was rescued from the lion's mouth.*" When you struggle, know that you have a God who will stand with you. You may feel alone, but you are not. Never forget the promise: "*Be strong and courageous. Do not fear or be in dread of them, for it is the* Lord *your God who goes with you. He will not leave you or forsake you*" (Deuteronomy 31:6). This is why we can joyfully say in the eye of the storm, "*For when I am weak, then I am strong*" (2 Corinthians 12:10). The more I am weakened, the more I must trust and rely on God. I stand on His Word more firmly when I cannot stand on my own.

"*He delivered us from such a deadly peril, and he will deliver us. On him we have set our hope that he will deliver us again*" (2 Corinthians 1:10). Have you noticed when God delivers and rescues you out of some great problem or difficulty, you have more confidence that He will help you again in the future? This is why you should make a commitment to be mentored by Christians who have known the Lord longer than you have. They are anchors in the storm. They have seen this before and they know God will deliver. This is precisely the tenor of Paul's message. This was not his "first rodeo" with suffering, nor would it be his final battle, but he was confident that God would keep on delivering him: "*He delivered...he will deliver... he will deliver us again*" (2 Corinthians 1:10). I hope you will appreciate the word picture of Paul's comment in verse 10, because it did not matter in which direction Paul looked in his life, God was always there delivering. When Paul looked back, God delivered; when he looked at present circumstances, God delivered; and if he looked forward at the mountain peaks to be traversed, "*he will deliver us again.*"

Make this your call to action today and every day of your walk with Christ. Commit to taking your eyes off of your pain and suffering and pointing your focus toward a God who delivers. Paul noticed God's grace inside and out, near and far, indeed, *everywhere*. Does this mean God will always deliver in the same way? No, it does not. Sometimes God will deliver us out of our suffering, while at other moments He will deliver us through the suffering. If God allows the death of a believer, we trust that His wisdom, plan, and timing are perfect. God will deliver in the way that only His omniscience knows. Our resolve is to trust Him.

Suffering Is Never in Vain; God's Plan Is Not Canceled by Trials

Paul never hesitated from asking his friends to pray for him: "*You also must help us by prayer, so that many will give thanks on our behalf for the blessing granted us through the prayers of many*" (2 Corinthians 1:11). Frequently throughout his letters, Paul specifically discussed his immediate need for their intercession and prayer: "*I appeal to you, brothers, by our Lord Jesus Christ and by the love of the Spirit, to strive together with me in your prayers to God on my behalf*" (Romans 15:30). There is a partnership in the body of Christ. We are a family in Christ. We can both pray and give thanks for each other. Notice Paul directed them to pray, give thanks, and *then* expect God to work deliverance. James tells us to expect trials, because suffering will always validate our faith: "*Count it all joy, my brothers, when you meet trials of various kinds, for you know that the testing of your faith produces steadfastness. And let steadfastness have its full effect, that you may be perfect and complete, lacking in nothing*" (James 1:2–4). The English word "*trials*" is *peirasmos* in the original Greek—*piracy* is also derived from this word. Trials are like invading raiders (pirates) in our lives. It is not "if" but "when" we face trials.

Interestingly, the verse most believers know about gaining wisdom (see James 1:5) is immediately preceded by the promise that trials of various kinds will come. We are to count it as all joy when trials do arrive, because "*blessed is the man who trusts in the Lord, whose trust is the Lord*" (Jeremiah 17:7). Our job is to be prepared for the "when" of trials by saturating our minds and hearts in God's Word and applying His "*great and precious promises*" (2 Peter 1:4 NIV) to each trial we face. Impressing God's Word on your heart will cause you to perform beyond your human ability and overcome your circumstances.

The cross is the greatest reminder of the unfailing love of God for mankind, which of course, means everyone. "*For God so loved the world*" (John 3:16) has no qualifiers. The resurrection of Jesus promises our ultimate victory. God is not finished with you. He can see the parade of your life—beginning, middle, and end. He is now working to rescue you from a world marred by sin, because He "*gave himself for our sins to deliver us from the present evil age*" (Galatians 1:4). I will never forget standing in the Mamertine Prison in Rome, where tradition says Paul spent his last days. Similar to a dungeon and Rome's version of death row, I thought of Paul's strength-through-God as a comfort for his suffering, even knowing the end was near. In the very cell I was standing, Paul wrote, "*For this reason I also suffer these things, but I am not ashamed; for I know whom I have believed and I am convinced that He is able to guard what I have entrusted to Him until that day*" (2 Timothy 1:12 NASB).

Only God can lead us to view our trials as temporary experiences, awful as they may be, and as preparation for the exceeding joy and glory of His eternal presence. The apostle Paul said that our present suffering is a "*light momentary affliction*" (2 Corinthians 4:17) that will last only a short time but will also serve to prepare us for the glory of heaven. From his prison cell Paul wrote to the persecuted church at Philippi, admonishing them to "*rejoice in the Lord always*" (Philippians 4:4).

19

ENGAGEMENT PRINCIPLE #5: AVOID ISLAND FEVER

A*wkward*. This is one of the most feared words among Christians who, try as they might, have great difficulty talking about Jesus with the world around them. Implementing leadership engagement principles cannot be done within the friendly confines of your own comfort zone. To be effective answering the unanswered questions of Christianity, we must be intentional about "burning the ships" of our comfort zone.

In 1519, the Spanish conquistador Hernán Cortés landed in Veracruz and became the first European to conquer Mexico. He famously commanded his troops to "burn the ships," because by doing so, retreat would no longer be an option. For Cortés, it was victory or death; there was no third way. Too many Christians have lived in an incubator within their personal comfort zone and, as a result, they are ineffective at engaging the world around them, let alone their own neighbors.

My wife and I have had our share of awkward experiences that have pushed us out of the nest of comfort and complacency in the Christian life. A few years ago, Audrey and I met with some missionary friends based in Dresden, Germany. It was a wonderful experience because we love Germany. German food is my favorite. My "Oma" and "Opa" are German, a few of my aunts were born in Germany, and I appreciate my German heritage. None of this prepared me for our experience with street evangelism on the Alaunstrasse, a few minutes outside the city center of Dresden. German youth are mobile. They use the ICE (Intercity-Express) rail system. Every weekend young German adults descend on the Alaunstrasse in Dresden for all-night partying and revelry. What is an otherwise quiet half-mile strip during the day becomes a non-stop party at night.

There we were at the south end of Alaunstrasse. Our missionary friend, Charlotte, dropped us (and a few others) off for some cold-turkey street evangelism. We divided into pairs. It was late in the evening and our goal was to make it to the north end of the street. My wife looked at me, realizing we did not have a translator. We looked up the street, breathed a prayer, and said, "Here we go!" By the time we reached the north end we had discussed Jesus with Satanists, drug users, atheists, and a host of other colorful youth. Most of them told us that they were atheists. You can imagine how far out of our comfort zone we felt. This experience was formative and helpful. I wish every Christian could be dropped off on the Alaunstrasse on the weekend. First, this experience was humbling. We realized that we did not know what we did not know. We needed to grow. Second, it was challenging and encouraging. We did not want to stay on the island of Christian comfort.

I am concerned about Christians isolating themselves into irrelevancy. Do you know how people who do not believe in Jesus think? Are you aware of the unanswered questions in the church? This principle of engagement encourages us to burn the ships to our isle of comfort and to invest ourselves in the world around us, uncomfortable as it may be at times. It is imperative that you understand culturally what is being said about Christianity in the world around you in order to effectively engage it.

Christianity has explanatory power. When you encounter challenges to the Christian faith, you will find that there *are* answers—*better* answers—that allay doubt and reinforce belief. The problem is that most Christians are unaware of opposition to their faith. Our job is to remove barriers to belief. This was the mission of Jesus' ministry. He opened the eyes of the spiritually blind. We are living in an increasingly hostile environment toward all things of faith. In a post-Christian era, a world in which it seems that Christianity already has "two strikes" against it, we must be committed to going the extra mile—venturing beyond the limits of our comfort zone and leaving behind our island of comfort. This final principle is simple, so much so that most people miss it. The social globalization of our world has caused cultures to blend and mix together conflated beliefs. There is much confusion. We cannot implement Engagement Principles 1–4 if we are not willing to escape the island of comfort in our Christian lives.

There are numerous helpful resources available designed to encourage you in your quest to avoid island fever in the Christian life. In my opinion, one of the most effective studies to energize you on your way to effective engagement is *Becoming a Contagious Christian* by Mark Mittelberg, Lee Strobel, and Bill Hybels.[143] The five engagement principles surveyed in *Unanswered* are designed as launching points, not as be-alls and end-alls. My prayer is that you will build your own list of effective leadership engagement principles as you seek to answer the unanswered questions of your faith.

MORE UNANSWERED QUESTIONS – I HOPE TO HEAR FROM YOU

Asking a question takes courage. It does not matter what your age is or what life situation you find yourself in, asking a question can be difficult—similar to trying to cap a volcano! Sooner or later, the questions are going to erupt. I encourage you to be open about your questions. As we have discovered in this book, many of the most important individuals in the Bible had gnawing questions—questions they needed answered before committing their lives! Others were passionately committed to God and still had questions (Job, Jesus, etc.).

Admitting doubt, desiring more information, believing based on evidence, doing due diligence; these are all important if not essential elements in making wise decisions. If I can help you in your journey of faith or if you are exploring the truth claims of Christianity, I hope to hear from you.

Please feel free to email me your *Unanswered* question:
ask@ChristianThinkers.com or tweet me at @JeremyJohnstonJ.

ENDNOTES

Chapter 1

1. Richard Bauckham, *Jesus: A Very Short Introduction* (Oxford: Oxford University Press, 2011), 1.
2. Amanda Petrusich, "Free To Be Miley," *Paper* (June 9, 2015). Available at: http://www.papermag.com/2015/06/miley_cyrus_happy_hippie_foundation.php.

Chapter 2

3. "Despair." www.MerriamWebster.com. Merriam-Webster, n. d. Web. 3 August 2015. http://www.merriam-webster.com/dictionary/despair.

4. Ludwig Koehler, Walter Baumgartner, Johann Jakob Stamm, and M. E. J. Richardson (translator), *The Hebrew and Aramaic Lexicon of the Old Testament,* vol. 1 (Leiden, Netherlands: Brill Academic Publishers, 1999).

Chapter 3

5. Herbert Lockyer, *All the Promises of the Bible* (Grand Rapids, MI: Zondervan, 1962), 9–12.

6. Oswald Chambers, *Daily Thoughts for Disciples* (Grand Rapids, MI: Zondervan, 1975), 75.

7. Warren Wiersbe, *Prayer 101: Experiencing the Heart of God* (Colorado Springs, CO: Victor, 2006), 75.

Chapter 4

8. R. J. Krejcir, "Statistics and Reasons for Church Decline," Francis A. Schaeffer Institute of Church Leadership Development (2007), www.intothyword.org/apps/articles/default.asp?articleid=36557&columnid=3958 (accessed January 30, 2012).

9. Alister McGrath, *C. S. Lewis – A Life: Eccentric Genius, Reluctant Prophet* (Carol Stream, IL: Tyndale House, 2013), 200–01.

10. C. S. Lewis and Lesley Walmsely (editor), *C. S. Lewis Essay Collection and Other Short Pieces* (London: HarperCollins, 2000), 155.

Chapter 5

11. Dominic Patten, "The Walking Dead Ratings Hit Season Finale Hit Season High With 15.8M Viewers." *Deadline* (March 30, 2015). Available at: http://deadline.com/2015/03/walking-dead-ratings-season-5-finale-record-1201400919/; see also Rick Kissell, 2015. "AMC's 'Walking Dead' Draws Record Finale Ratings." Available at: http://variety.com/2015/tv/news/amcs-walking-dead-draws-record-finale-ratings-1201462598/.

12. Jonathan Mahler and Bill Carter, "Series is On, and Everybody's Watching…Football." *New York Times* (October 24, 2014). Available at: *http*://www.nytimes.com/2014/10/24/sports/baseball/world-series-2014-baseball-is-no-longer-center-of-attention-in-new-landscape.html?_r=0.

13. Cork Gaines, "Chart: TV Ratings For The NBA Finals Are The Worst In 5 Years," *Business Insider* (June 18, 2013). Available at: *http*://www.businessinsider.com/chart-tv-ratings-for-the-nba-finals-are-the-worst-in-5-years-2013-6.

14. Erica Phillips, "Zombie Studies Gain Ground on College Campuses," *The Wall Street Journal* (March 3, 2014). Available at: http://www.wsj.com/articles/SB10001424052702304851104579361451951384512?cb=logged0.8001834866590798.

15. N. T. Wright, *The Resurrection of the Son of God: Christian Origins and the Question of God*, vol 3 (Minneapolis, MN: Fortress Press, 2003), 35. Wright replies to Stanley E. Porter, "Resurrection, the Greeks and the New Testament," in S. E. Porter, M. A. Hayes, and D. Tombs (eds.), *Resurrection* (JSNTSup 186; RILP 5; Sheffield: Sheffield Academic Press, 1999), 52–81. Porter explores what evidence there is of Greco-Roman beliefs about the afterlife. Wright notes that none of it approaches the Jewish understanding of resurrection. In fairness to Porter, his principal point was to note that not all afterlife ideas in Greek thought were purely spiritual.

16. At several points I depend on the forthcoming work by C. A. Evans, *Jesus and the Remains of His Day* (Peabody, MA: Hendrickson). I thank Professor Evans for making his work available. To study beliefs in ghosts from the time of Jesus see: D. Felton, *Haunted Greece and Rome: Ghost Stories from Classical Antiquity* (Austin, TX: University of Texas Press, 1999); L. Collison-Morley, *Greek and Roman Ghost Stories* (Oxford: Blackwell, 1912).

17. See the story of Odysseus's sailor who terrorized the people of Temesa: W. H. S. Jones, *Pausanius Description of Greece* III (LCL 272; Cambridge, MA: Harvard University Press; London: Heinemann, 1988) 39, 41.

18. Felton, *Haunted Greece and Rome,* 10, 103 n. 56.

19. Translation based on J. C. Rolfe, *Suetonius,* vol. I (Cambridge, MA: Harvard University Press, 1998) 505, 507.

20. The resurrection is mocked and attacked by other thinkers from late antiquity, whose views can be found in the writings of several Fathers of the Church (see Gregory of Nyssa, *Catechetical Oration* 5; Lactantius, *Institutes* 4.16, 5.2; and Libanius, *Oration* 18.178 see also the pagan perspective in Lucian, *Peregrinus* 11).

21. *Origen, Contra Celsum,* preface 1–4. For the critical edition, see Henry Chadwick, *Origen: Contra Celsum* (Cambridge: Cambridge University, 1953). *On the True Doctrine* has been reconstructed from *Contra Celsum* by R. Joseph Hoffmann, Celsus, *On the True Doctrine* (New York: Oxford University Press, 1987). On Celsus, see E. R. Dodds, *Pagan and Christian in an Age of Anxiety* (Cambridge: Cambridge University, 1965), 116–21. Hoffmann, *Celsus,* 61–62, 67–69; *Origen, Contra Celsum* 2.54, 59–75. Sceptics like Celsus reasoned, in the words of Vaganay: Qui donc avait vu de ses yeux le Christ au moment de sa resurrection? Personne. ("Who then saw Christ with their own eyes at the moment of his resurrection? No one."); Hoffmann, *Celsus,* 61–62, 67–69; *Origen, Contra Celsum* 2.54, 59–75. Sceptics like Celsus reasoned, in the words of Vaganay: Qui donc avait vu de ses yeux le Christ au moment de sa resurrection? Personne. ("Who then saw Christ with their own eyes at the moment of his resurrection? No one").

22. Craig A. Evans, Jeremiah J. Johnston, "Resurrection," *Oxford Encyclopedia of Bible and Ethics,* vol 2, Robert L. Brawley (ed.) (Oxford: Oxford University Press, 2014) 208–212.

23. http://www.al.com/living/index.ssf/2013/03/easter_ranks_first_in_church_a.html.

24. For a detailed daily Bible study on the resurrection of Jesus, see my associated study, Jeremiah J. Johnston, *Unanswered: Lasting Truth for Trending Questions* (Nashville: LifeWay Publishing), 2015.

25. Paul Sangster, *Doctor Sangster* (London: The Epworth Press, 1962), 127.
26. Ibid., 195.
27. Ibid., 347.
28. Ibid., 149.
29. Ibid., 202.
30. Ibid., 360.
31. Ibid., 346.
32. Ibid., 341.
33. Ibid., 359.
34. Ibid.
35. Ibid., 333.
36. April AD 33 is also an alternative date for the crucifixion of Jesus. For a more detailed analysis of the dating of Jesus death and resurrection, see Robert H. Stein, *Jesus the Messiah: A Survey of the Life of Christ* (Downers Grove, IL; Leicester, England: InterVarsity Press, 1996), 59.

Chapter 6

37. Honor Whiteman, "CDC: life expectancy in the US reaches record high," *Medical News Today* (October 8, 2014). Available at: http://www.medicalnewstoday.com/articles/283625.php; Larry Copeland, "Life expectancy in the USA hits a record high," *USA Today* (October 9, 2014). Available at: http://www.usatoday.com/story/news/nation/2014/10/08/us-life-expectancy-hits-record-high/16874039/.
38. Sarah Kliff, "The U.S. ranks 26th for life expectancy, right behind Slovenia," *The Washington Post* (November 21, 2013). Available at: http://www.washingtonpost.com/blogs/wonkblog/wp/2013/11/21/the-u-s-ranks-26th-for-life-expectancy-right-behind-slovenia/; see also "U.S. Life Expectancy Ranks 26th In The World, OECD Report Shows. *Huffington Post* (November 21,

2013). Available at: http://www.huffingtonpost.com/2013/11/21/us-life-expectancy-oecd_n_4317367.html.

39. Edwin M. Yamauchi, Marvin R. Wilson, *Dictionary of Daily Life in Biblical & Post-Biblical Antiquity*, vol 1 (Peabody, MA: Hendrickson, 2014), 285.
40. Ibid., 204.
41. Ibid., 285.
42. For detailed discussion of Jesus' kingdom proclamation, see Jeremiah J. Johnston and C. A. Evans, "Kingdom of God/Heaven," *The Oxford Encyclopedia of Bible and Theology*, edited by Samuel E. Balentine, et al. (Oxford and New York: Oxford University Press, 2014); Jeremiah J. Johnston and C. A. Evans, "Kingdom of God," in *Encyclopedia of Early Christianity*, edited by Paul J.J. van Geest, Bert Jan Lietaert Peerbolte, David Hunter (Leiden, Netherlands: Brill Academic Publishers, 2015).
43. Bernard Green, *Christianity in Ancient Rome: The First Three Centuries* (London: T&T Clark, 2010), 17.
44. Ibid., 177.
45. Ibid., 170.

Chapter 7

46. http://www.nfl.com/videos/nfl-cant-miss-plays/09000d5d81d8d049/Wild-Card-Can-t-Miss-Play-Lynch-in-beast-mode.
47. http://www.seahawks.com/news/2015/01/08/date-marshawn-lynch's-beast-mode-run-makes-earth-and-saints-quake.
48. http://thesportsdaily.net/marshawn-lynch-reveals-the-meaning-behind-his-beast-mode-nickname-video/.
49. http://thesportsdaily.net/marshawn-lynch-reveals-the-meaning-behind-his-beast-mode-nickname-video/.

Chapter 8

50. Ken Camp, "Denominational Leader, Pastor Phil Lineberger dead at 69," *Baptist News Global* (June 2, 2015). Available at: https://baptistnews.com/ministry/people/item/30138-denominational-leader-pastor-phil-lineberger-dead-at-69.

51. Cherese Jackson, "Another Pastor Commits Suicide," *Liberty Voice* (April 19, 2014). Available at: www.guardianlv.com/2014/04/another-pastor-commits-suicide.

52. Amber Phillips, "Joe Biden's heartfelt speech on grief," *The Washington Post* (May 31, 2015). Available at: http://www.washingtonpost.com/blogs/the-fix/wp/2015/05/31/joe-bidens-heartfelt-thoughts-on-grief/?tid=sm_tw.

53. "First WHO World Suicide Report," *World Health Organization*. Available at: http://www.who.int/mental_health/suicide-prevention/en/.

54. Justin Worland, "This Bill Could Help Veterans With Mental Health," *Time* (February 6, 2015). Available at: http://time.com/3694053/veteran-suicide/.

55. Alison Bruzek, "Suicides Rise In Middle-Aged Men, And Older Men Remain At Risk," *NPR* (September 10, 2014). Available at: http://www.npr.org/sections/health-shots/2014/09/10/347386843/suicides-rise-in-middle-aged-men-and-older-men-remain-at-risk.

56. Stephen Altrogge, "Is Mental Illness Actually Biblical?" *Bible Study Tools*. Available at: http://www.biblestudytools.com/blogs/stephen-altrogge/is-mental-illness-actually-biblical.html.

57. Matthew Stucker, "Robin Williams' death ruled suicide," CNN (November 11, 2014). Available at: www.cnn.com/2014/11/07/showbiz/robin-williams-autopsy.

58. These questions are adapted from the San Francisco Suicide Prevention *Myth's and Facts* webpage: http://www.sfsuicide.org/prevention-strategies/myths-and-facts/.

59. Alan Duke, "Rick Warren's son lost in 'wave of despair'," *CNN* (April 8, 2013). Available at: http://www.cnn.com/2013/04/07/us/matthew-warren-suicide.

Chapter 9

60. Amy Morin, "How To Foster Good Mental Health In The Workplace," *Forbes* (April 9, 2015). Available at: www.forbes.com/sites/amymorin/2015/04/09/how-to-foster-good-mental-health-in-the-workplace/?utm_campaign=Forbes&utm_source=TWITTER&utm_medium=social&utm_channel=Entrepreneurs&linkId=13436828.

61. Marina Marcus, M. Taghi Yasamy, Mark van Ommeren, Dan Chisholm, Shekhar Saxena (WHO Department of Mental Health and Substance Abuse), "Depression: A Global Public Health Concern" (2012). Available at: http://www.who.int/mental_health/management/depression/who_paper_depression_wfmh_2012.pdf.

62. Ronald C. Kessler, Ph.D.; Katherine A. McGonagle, Ph.D.; Shanyang Zhao, Ph.D.; Christopher B. Nelson, M.P.H.; Michael Hughes, Ph.D.; Suzann Eshleman, M.A.; Hans-Ulrich Wittchen, Ph.D.; Kenneth S. Kendler, M.D., "Lifetime and 12-Month Prevalence of DSM-III-R Psychiatric Disorders in the United States: Results From the National Comorbidity Survey," *Arch Gen Psychiatry*. 1994;51(1):8–19. Available at: http://apsychoserver.psych.arizona.edu/JJBAReprints/PSYC621/Kessler%20et%20al_Lifetime%20and%2012%20months%20prevalence_Archives%20of%20Gen%20Psychiatry_%60994.pdf.

63. Diane Coutu, "High-Pressure Jobs and Mental Illness," *Harvard Business Review* (April 2, 2015). Available at: https://hbr.org/2015/04/high-pressure-jobs-and-mental-illness.

64. Ruby Wax, "What's So Funny About Mental Illness?" *TED* (posted October 2012). Available at: http://www.ted.com/talks/ruby_wax_what_s_so_funny_about_mental_illness?language=en.

65. Staff, 2015. "Mental Health and The Church." *Leadership Network*. Available at: http://leadnet.org/mental-health-summit/.

66. William Cowper, John Newton, "God Moves in a Mysterious Way," 1774.

Chapter 10

67. Peter Bregman, "If You Want People To Listen, Stop Talking," *Harvard Business Review* (May 25, 2015). Available at: https://hbr.org/2015/05/if-you-want-people-to-listen-stop-talking.

Chapter 11

68. John Horn, "The haunted history of 'Paranormal Activity'," *Los Angeles Times* (September 20, 2009). Available at: http://articles.latimes.com/2009/sep/20/entertainment/ca-paranormal20.

69. Ibid.

70. Owen Gleiberman, "'Paranormal Activity': A marketing campaign so ingenious it's scary," *Entertainment Weekly* (October 7, 2009). Available at: http://www.ew.com/article/2009/10/07/paranormal-activity-marketing-campaign.

71. Dorothy Pomerantz, "The Triumph Of 'Paranormal Activity'," *Forbes* (October 18, 2012). Available at: http://www.forbes.com/sites/dorothypomerantz/2012/10/18/the-triumph-of-paranormal-activity/; Eric Ditzian, "'Paranormal Activity' Is Most Profitable Film Of All-Time." *MTV News* (October 29, 2009). Available at: http://www.mtv.com/news/1625095/paranormal-activity-is-most-profitable-film-of-all-time/.

72. Richard Lacayo, "Step Right Up," *Time* (March 10, 1997), 34.

73. David Robson, "Psychology: The truth about the paranormal," *BBC Future* (October 31, 2014). Available at: http://www.bbc.com/future/story/20141030-the-truth-about-the-paranormal.

74. Esther Inglis-Arkell, "When Churchill met Lincoln. Naked," *IO9* (October 28, 2011). Available at: http://io9.com/5852898/when-churchill-met-lincoln-naked.

75. Benjamin Radford, "Are Ghosts Real? Science Says No-o-o-o," *Live Science* (October 21, 2014). Available at http://www.livescience.com/26697-are-ghosts-real.html.

76. Christopher Bader, Carson Mencken, and Joseph Baker, *Paranormal America* (New York: New York University Press, 2010), 52.

77. Ibid., 72–73.

78. Donna Anderson, "Survey Reveals That 70 to 80 Percent of Americans Believe in Paranormal Activity," *Examiner* (November 5, 2010). Available at: http://www.examiner.com/article/survey-reveals-that-70-to-80-percent-of-americans-believe-paranormal-activity.

79. Jake Flanagin, "There Is a Paranormal Activity Lab at the University of Virginia," *The Atlantic* (February 10, 2014). Available at: http://www.theatlantic.com/health/archive/2014/02/there-is-a-paranormal-activity-lab-at-the-university-of-virginia/283584/.

80. Ibid., *Paranormal America,* 73, 107.

81. Staff statistics. *American Federation of Certified Psychics and Mediums, Inc.* Available at: http://www.americanfederationofcertifiedpsychicsandmediums.org/statistics.htm.

82. Ibid.

83. Ibid.

84. "New Research Explores Teenage Views and Behavior Regarding the Supernatural," *Barna Group* (January 23, 2006). Available at: https://www.barna.org/barna-update/article/5-barna-update/164-new-research-explores-teenage-views-and-behavior-regarding-the-supernatural#.VYcpqmBJfGt.

85. Jeremiah J. Johnston, C. A. Evans, "Kingdom of God/Heaven"; Jeremiah J. Johnston and C. A. Evans, "Kingdom of God."

Chapter 12

86. Alister McGrath, *C. S. Lewis: A Life* (Carol Stream, IL: Tyndale House, 2013), 216.

87. Ibid, 217.

88. C. S. Lewis, *The Screwtape Letters* (New York: HarperOne, 2009), IX.

89. Merrill F. Unger, *Biblical Demonology* (Grand Rapids, MI: Kregel Publications, 1994), 62.

90. Charles Spurgeon, *Charles Spurgeon: Lectures to My Students,* vol. 2 (Huntington, DE: Delmarva Publications, Inc., 2015).

91. William Gurnall, *The Christian in Complete Armour,* vol. 1 (London: Blackie and Son, 1865), 22.

92. Ibid., 101, 266.

Chapter 14

93. Daniel Radish, "The Good Book Business," *The New Yorker* (December 18, 2006). Available at: http://www.newyorker.com/magazine/2006/12/18/the-good-book-business.

94. Stevenson Swanson, "Bible sells big, so do its spinoffs," *Chicago Tribune* (June 4, 2007). Available at: http://articles.chicagotribune.com/2007-06-04/news/0706030703_1_religious-publishers-book-industry-study-group-bible-publisher.

95. Barna Group, American Bible Society: *State of the Bible 2015* (New York: American Bible Society/Barna Group, 2015) 20. Available at: http://www.americanbible.org/features/state-of-the-bible-2015.

96. A. C. Grayling, *The Good Book: A Humanist Bible* (New York: Walker & Co., 2011).

97. Ibid., dust jacket copy.

98. Barna Group, *State of the Bible 2015,* 5.

99. Ibid., 18.

100. Ibid., 27.

101. Ibid.

102. Ibid., 12.

103. Ibid., 11.

104. Idid., 13.

105. Ibid.

106. Ibid., 24.

107. Ibid., 13.

108. Ibid., 6.

109. Ibid., 10.

110. James Penner, Rachel Harder, Erika Anderson, Bruno Desorcy, and Rick Hiemstra, "Hemorrhaging Faith: Why & When Canadian Young Adults are Leaving, Staying & Returning to the Church" (Commissioned by EFC Youth and Young Adult Ministry Roundtable, 2013).

111. Trevor Grundy, "Survey finds British children and adults are biblically illiterate," *Religion News Service* (February 7, 2014). Available at: http://www.religionnews.com/2014/02/07/survey-finds-british-children-adults-biblically-illiterate/.

112. Ibid.

113. Stacey Bredhoff, *American Originals* (Seattle, WA: The University of Washington Press, 2001) 52. Available at: http://www.ourdocuments.gov/doc.php?flash=true&doc=38.

114. Mark A. Noll, *The Civil War as a Theological Crisis* (Chapel Hill, NC: The University of North Carolina Press, 2015 reprint).

115. Fox News report based on: Michelle Jamrisko, "Americans' Spending on Dining Out Just Overtook Grocery Sales for the First Time Ever," *Bloomberg Business* (April 14, 2015). Available at: http://www.bloomberg.com/news/articles/2015-04-14/americans-spending-on-dining-out-just-overtook-grocery-sales-for-the-first-time-ever.

116. For a comprehensive assessment of the Islamic State, see: Craig A. Evans and Jeremiah J. Johnston, *Jesus and the Jihadis* (Shippensburg, PA: Destiny Image Publishing, 2015).

117. Thankful to my friend, Professor Paul Maier, for sharing this helpful information at a Christian Thinkers Society conference.

118. For a comprehensive biography of Luther's life, see: Roland Bainton, *Here I Stand* (Nashville: Abingdon, 2013); for helpful summaries, see: Stephen Nichols, *Martin Luther: A Guided Tour of His Life and Thought* (Phillipsburg, NJ: P&R Publishing Company, 2002); Graham Tomlin, *Luther & His World* (Oxford: Lion Books, 2002).

119. Martin Luther, *Luther's Works, 33: Career of the Reformer III* (Minneapolis, MN: Fortress Press, 1972).

120. http://everything2.com/title/Imperial+Edict+of+Worms. (Accessed 28 July, 2015.)

121. Martin Marty, *Martin Luther: A Life* (New York: Penguin Books, 2004), 71.

122. Harold Rawlings, *Trial by Fire* (Wellington, FL: The Rawlings Foundation, 2004), 75.

123. Martin Luther, *Luther's Works, Vol. 54: Table Talk,* edited by Jaroslav Jan Pelikan, Hilton C. Oswald, and Helmut T. Lehmann (St. Louis, MO: Concordia Publishing House, 1999), 165.

124. Max DePree, *Leadership Is an Art* (New York: Crown Business, 2004), 11.

Chapter 15

125. Rawlings, *Trial By Fire,* 103.

126. Owen Jarus, "Mummy Mask May Contain Oldest Known Gospel," *Live Science* (January 18, 2015). Available at: http://www.livescience.com/49489-oldest-known-gospel-mummy-mask.html.

127. For an excellent book that will inspire you to go deeper in your spiritual disciplines, see Philip Nation, *Habits for our Holiness: How the Spiritual Disciplines Grow Us Up, Draw Us Together, and Send Us Out* (Chicago: Moody Publishers, 2016).
128. Presbyterian Church in the U.S.A. Board of Publication, *Publications,* Issue 102 (1842) 276.
129. David Danielle, *William Tyndale: A Biography* (New Haven and London: Yale University Press, 1994), 365.
130. Ibid., 365.
131. Ibid., 384.
132. "William Tyndale's New Testament." *The British Library.* Available at: http://www.bl.uk/onlinegallery/onlineex/landprint/tyndale/.
133. Ibid.
134. I am especially thankful to Dr. Diana Severance, curator of the Dunham Bible Museum at Houston Baptist University, for her tireless efforts to tell the story of the Bible. Her advocacy for the Bible has influenced me and I share her enthusiasm for a greater awareness of the story of the Bible; I also am thankful to my friend, Dr. Harold Rawlings, who shortly after I became a minister, preached on a number of occasions at the church where I was on staff, and opened our eyes to the story of the English Bible, with his priceless Bible collection.
135. "Holy Bible, book divine." Hymnary.org. Available at: http://www.hymnary.org/text/holy_bible_book_divine.

Chapter 17

136. Ralph P. Martin, *Word Biblical Commentary, Vol. 40, 2 Corinthians* (Nashville, TN: Thomas Nelson, 1985), 140.
137. Randy Alcorn, *If God Is Good* (Colorado Springs, CO: Multnomah, 2010), 4.
138. Kevin Belmonte, *D. L. Moody–A Life: Innovator, Evangelist, World Changer* (Chicago, IL: Moody Publishers, 2014), 102.

Chapter 18

139. Walter Isaacson, *Steve Jobs* (New York: Simon & Schuster, 2011), 14.

140. C. S. Lewis, *Mere Christianity* (New York: Macmillan Publishing, 1952), 45–46.

141. Arnold A. Dallimore, *Spurgeon: A New Biography* (Edinburgh: Banner of Truth, 1985), 176.

142. Joel C. Gregory, *Growing Pains of the Soul* (Nashville, TN: Thomas Nelson, 1987), 13.

Chapter 19

143. Mark Mittleberg, Lee Strobel, and Bill Hybels, *Becoming a Contagious Christian* (Grand Rapids, MI: Zondervan, 1996, 2007).

SUGGESTED READING

Chapter 1: Questions Have Power

Lee Strobel, *The Case for Faith: A Journalist Investigates the Toughest Objections to Christianity* (Grand Rapids, MI: Zondervan, 2014).

Timothy Keller, *The Reason for God: Belief in an Age of Skepticism* (New York: Dutton, 2008).

David Limbaugh, *Jesus on Trial: A Lawyer Affirms the Truth of the Gospel* (Washington, DC: Regnery, 2014).

William Lane Craig, *Reasonable Faith: Christian Truth and Apologetics*, 3rd ed. (Wheaton, IL: Crossway, 2008).

Alvin J. Schmidt, *How Christianity Changed the World* (Grand Rapids, MI: Zondervan, 2004).

Chapter 2: Come Out, Come Out, Wherever You Are, God

Gary R. Habermas, *Why Is God Ignoring Me?: What to Do When It Feels Like He's Giving You the Silent Treatment* (Carol Stream, IL: Tyndale House, 2010).

Andreas Köstenberger, Darrell Bock, and Josh Chatraw, *Truth Matters: Confident Faith in a Confusing World* (Nashville, TN: B&H Academic, 2014).

Jefferson Bethke, *Jesus > Religion: Why He Is So Much Better Than Trying Harder, Doing More, and Being Good Enough* (Nashville, TN: Thomas Nelson, 2013).

Chapter 3: Anticipating the Savior in the Silence

Ravi Zacharias, *Has Christianity Failed You?* (Grand Rapids, MI: Zondervan, 2010).

Ron Rhodes, *Answering the Objections of Atheists, Agnostics & Skeptics* (Eugene, OR: Harvest House, 2006).

Jan Harrison, *Life after the Storm: God Will Carry You Through* (Eugene, OR: Harvest House, 2015).

Chapter 4: Being a Channel, Not a Resevoir

Lee Strobel, *The Case for Grace: A Journalist Explores the Evidence of Transformed Lives* (Grand Rapids, MI: Zondervan, 2015).

Paul Copan, *That's Just Your Interpretation: Responding to Skeptics Who Challenge Your Faith* (Grand Rapids, MI: Baker Books, 2001).

Andreas Kostenberger, Darrell Bock, and Josh Chatraw, *Truth in a Culture of Doubt: Engaging Skeptical Challenges to the Bible* (Nashville, TN: B&H Academic, 2014).

Chapter 5: The Dead Rise

Lee Strobel, *The Case for the Resurrection: A First-Century Investigative Reporter Probes History's Pivotal Event* (Grand Rapids, MI: Zondervan, 2008).

Richard Bauckham, *Jesus and the Eyewitnesses: The Gospels as Eyewitness Testimony* (Grand Rapids, MI: Eerdmans Publishing, Co., 2006).

Craig A. Evans, *Fabricating Jesus: How Modern Scholars Distort the Gospels* (Downers Grove, IL: IVP Books, 2006).

Lee Strobel, *The Case for the Real Jesus: A Journalist Investigates Current Attacks on the Identity of Christ* (Grand Rapids, MI: Zondervan, 2007).

Craig A. Evans, *Jesus and His World: The Archaeological Evidence* (Louisville, KY: Westminster John Knox Press, 2013).

Paul L. Maier, *In the Fullness of Time: A Historian Looks at Christmas, Easter, and the Early Church* (Grand Rapids, MI: Kregel Publications, 1997).

Dinesh D'Souza, *What's So Great about Christianity* (Washington, DC: Regnery, 2007).

W. Mark Lanier, *Christianity on Trial: A Lawyer Examines the Christian Faith* (Downers Grove, IL: IVP Books, 2014).

Adrian Warnock, *Raised with Christ: How the Resurrection Changes Everything* (Wheaton, IL: Crossway, 2009).

Chapter 6: Evidence of the Greatest Comeback Ever

Lee Strobel, *The Case for Christ: A Journalist's Personal Investigation of the Evidence for Jesus* (Grand Rapids, MI: Zondervan, 1998).

Craig A. Evans and N. T. Wright, *Jesus, the Final Days: What Really Happened* (Louisville, KY: Westminster John Knox, 2009).

David Skeel, *True Paradox: How Christianity Makes Sense of Our Complex World* (Downers Grove, IL: IVP Books, 2014).

Hank Hanegraaff, *Resurrection: The Capstone in the Arch of Christianity* (Nashville, TN: Thomas Nelson, 2002).

Mark Mittelberg, *The Questions Christians Hope No One Will Ask* (Carol Stream, IL: Tyndale House, 2010).

Chapter 8: Elephant in the Room

Jerry Johnston, *Why Suicide?* (Nashville, TN: Thomas Nelson, 1987).

Chapter 9: "Please Leave Our Church" and Other Disasters

Anna Tague's blog: *Living Hope Recovery.* http://living-hope-recovery.weebly.com/.

Chapter 11: Vampires, Zombies, Ghosts, Mediums, and Paranormal Phenomenon Have Never Been More Normal or Profitable

Ron Rhodes, *The Truth Behind Ghosts, Mediums and Psychic Phenomena* (Eugene, OR: Harvest House, 2006).

Kristine McGuire, *Escaping the Cauldron: Exposing Occult Influences in Everyday Life* (Lake Mary, FL: Charisma House, 2012).

Richard Wiseman, *Paranormality: Why We See What Isn't There* (Spin Solutions Ltd., 2011).

Chapter 12: He Who Is in Me Is Greater Than He Who Is in the World

Walter Martin, *The Kingdom of the Occult*, Jill Martin Rische and Kurt Van Gorden, eds. (Nashville, TN: Thomas Nelson, 2008).

William Gurnall, *The Christian in Complete Armour (Volumes 1–3)*, abridged by Ruthanne Garlock, Kay King, Karen Sloan and Candy Coan. (Carlisle, PA: The Banner of Truth Trust, 1986).

Chapter 15: Until Heaven and Earth Pass Away

Neil R. Lightfoot, *How We Got the Bible*, third edition (Grand Rapids, MI: Baker Books, 2003).

Craig L. Blomberg, *Can We Still Believe the Bible?: An Evangelical Engagement with Contemporary Questions* (Grand Rapids, MI: Brazos Press, 2014).

F. F. Bruce, *The New Testament Documents: Are They Reliable?* (Grand Rapids, MI: Eerdmans Publishing Co., 1981).

Darrell L. Bock and Daniel B. Wallace, *Dethroning Jesus: Exposing Culture's Quest to Unseat the Biblical Christ* (Nashville, TN: Thomas Nelson, 2007).

Michael Bird, Craig A. Evans, Simon Gathercole, Charles E. Hill, and Chris Tilling, *How God Became Jesus: The Real Origins of Belief in Jesus' Divine Nature—A Response to Bart D. Ehrman* (Grand Rapids, MI: Zondervan, 2014).

Chapter 17: Prevent Faith

J. B. Phillips, *The Price of Success* (Wheaton, IL: Shaw Books, 1984).

Vera Phillips and Edwin Robertson, *The Wounded Healer— J. B. Phillips* (London: Triangle, 1984).

Chapter 18: The Problem of Love

Rodney Stark, *The Triumph of Christianity: How the Jesus Movement Became the World's Largest Religion* (New York: HarperOne, 2011).

Rodney Stark, *Cities of God: The Real Story of How Christianity Became an Urban Movement and Conquered Rome* (New York: HarperOne, 2006).

Craig A. Evans, *God Speaks: What He Says, What He Means* (Nashville, TN: Worthy Publishing, 2015).

ABOUT THE AUTHOR

Dr. Jeremiah J. Johnston is a New Testament scholar, professor, apologist, and regular speaker on university campuses, churches, and conferences. His passion is equipping Christians to give intellectually informed accounts of what they believe. Dr. Johnston completed his doctoral residency in Oxford in partnership with Oxford Centre for Mission Studies and received his Ph.D. from Middlesex University (United Kingdom), with commendation. He has Masters Degrees from Acadia University (Canada) and Midwestern Baptist Theological Seminary (US). He has lectured throughout the United States, Canada, and the United Kingdom.

In addition to his popular publications, Dr. Johnston has distinguished himself with publications in scholarly, refereed journals and serials. These include entries in Oxford University Press and E. J. Brill reference works. He specializes in Christian origins, Jesus and the Gospels, and topics, especially apologetics, that closely relate to Jesus and the Gospels. These include: the resurrection of Jesus, New Testament manuscripts (their number, nature, and reliability), extra-canonical gospels, resurrection, and afterlife beliefs. He has presented academic papers at learned meetings and has examined ancient texts (papyri, codices, and the like) at renowned libraries, such as the Griffith Papyrology Room of Oxford University's Bodleian Library and the Beinecke Rare Book and Manuscript Library of Yale University. Dr. Johnston co-edits an academic series for Bloomsbury T&T Clark and is currently preparing a volume on Jesus in Cambridge University Press's distinguished "In Context" series.

Dr. Johnston serves as the founder and president of Christian Thinkers Society, a resident institute at Houston Baptist University, where he also serves as associate professor of Early Christianity. Christian Thinkers Society produces live events, media productions, conferences, and publications to teach pastors and Christians to become thinkers, and thinkers to become Christians. Dr. Johnston resides in Houston, Texas, with his wife and two children.

For more information,

visit www.ChristianThinkers.com.

Connect with Jeremiah at:

Twitter: @JeremyJohnstonJ

Facebook: www.Facebook.com/ChristianThinkersSociety

Instagram: Jeremy_J_Johnston

If your group enjoyed *Unanswered*, help us tell the world about it. Take a few moments to tweet, like, post, pin, and otherwise share the love in all your social media channels.

- Here are a few tweets to consider:
  "I recommend reading #Unanswered by Jeremiah Johnston @WhitakerHouse"

  "My questions are no longer #Unanswered. Check out the new book from @JeremyJohnstonJ"

  "Got questions? See how Christianity intersects with tough issues like suicide, ghosts, and more in #Unanswered from @JeremyJohnstonJ"
- Head over to facebook.com/whitakerhouse, "LIKE" the page, and post a comment as to what you enjoyed the most.
- Pick up a copy for someone you know who would be challenged and encouraged by this message.
- Write a book review online.

#ChristianThinkersSociety

Visit these site for more great information.

whpub.me/un_answered

christianthinkers.com